# What's On Your Mind?

*A Guide to Biblical Ethics*

## by Dr. Michael Cephas, Sr.

Unless otherwise noted, Scripture quotations are from the King James Version of the Bible
Copyright © 1996
Broadman & Holman Publishers


Printed in the U.S.A. by
Lulu Enterprises
860 Aviaton Parkway
Morrisville, North Carolina 27560


Additional copies of this book are available by mail.
Send $20.95 each (includes tax and postage) to:
The New True Church of Jesus Christ
4991 Cleves Warsaw Pike
Cincinnati, Oh 45238
(513) 381-0727

**ISBN: 978-0-557-01879-6**

# Table of contents

*Dedication*
*Foreword – by Bishop D. Sorrells, Th.D, D.D., Ph.D*
*Introduction*
*My Story*

# Dedication

This book is dedicated to the memory of Bishop Dr. John T Cohen who taught and gave me the knowledge and wisdom down through the years. Even in his death he is still my pastor and is still preaching and teaching through me.

This book is also dedicated to my family and church family of The New True Church of the Apostolic Faith, Inc. who sat so patiently and heard the teaching before it became a book. To my lovely wife, First Lady Venita A. Cephas, who supports my vision in every aspect. To my daughter, Erica, who gave her time endlessly to help write this book. Thank you very much.

To Bishop Donald D. Sorrells, pastor of Christ Temple Apostolic Faith Church and CEO and Founder of the accredited Christ Temple Apostolic Bible Institute, who inspired and encouraged me to write this book.

# The Foreword

The commandment of Jesus written in St. Matthew 28:19 still echoes loud today, even in this twenty first century. "Go ye therefore and teach all nations baptizing them in the name of the Father, and of the Son, and of the Holy Ghost." Peter stood up on the Day of Pentecost and preached Jesus Christ, which was the fulfillment of the Great Commission, Acts 2:38.

In his book, Dr. Michael Cephas shows how God is able today to reach anyone, regardless of their situation in life, and save them and give them new direction in this present world.

Dr. Cephas has a great love for the youth of today, and understands the many pressures of being young. Therefore, he has taken the task of putting forth this book that he might pass on to this generation, the power of a blessed saviour and god, Jesus Christ.

Bishop D. Sorrells, Th.D, D.D., Ph.D
Founder & President
Christ Temple Apostolic Bible College

# Introduction

In writing this book I want to bring out the thoughts and things that have been plaguing the human family ever since the world began and man was created. In Genesis 4:1-10 we find that Cain was jealous of his brother so he killed him because he had a better sacrifice than he did..

There are many examples in the Bible of men and women being angry with one another. The purpose of this book is to show those who have suffered and dealt with anger in their life from their childhood on up to their adulthood that they can be healed and delivered from these works of the mind. In the Bible we read in Ecclesiastes 7:9, "Be not hasty in thy spirit to be angry: for anger resteth in the bosom of fools." The devil has caused humanity to be angry against one another. God commanded us to love and be at peace with one another. That is why I have written this book to show what is in man and how to get it out. This book also helps us to get to the root of the matter, which are the things that happened in our childhood that has made us bitter. The root of the matter is bitterness.

# My Story

It all started when I was twelve years old. I always heard my mother and father arguing over money and his constant absence in our lives. Not having a father in my life created a resentment and anger that spilled over into my adulthood. I did not know that it was wrong to feel that way, but I felt that way toward my father and the dysfunction in our home. Like any child, you want both parents in the home, but we didn't have that. This dysfunction affected my ability to function properly in school. It almost damaged my self esteem and character. When I got married and saved at the age of eighteen, the anger was still there. Even after ten years of marriage nothing had changed. I was still angry at my father for not being there for me.

One day I was at home cooking in the kitchen and I received a phone call and to my surprise it was my father asking me to help him. I thought to myself, "He has a whole lot of nerve to call me after all these years." I didn't want to help him because I was still angry with him for all the years he missed in my life. I went to my pastor, Bishop Dr. John T. Cohen and sat down and talked to him about what happened. I told him that I didn't really need my father, but in reality I did. My anger was telling me, "Why should I help him when he was never around when I needed him?" As I sat across the desk from my pastor, I began to cry because I realized that even at the age of thirty-eight years old I needed him. I thank God that my heart is fixed now. I will be fifty years old this year and I love my father, even in his grave. For the last three years before he passed away he was able to see me preach, teach and become his pastor. I was actually happy to know that my father was there. I thank God for the opportunity to re-establish a relationship with him before he passed.

# It's Not What Goes In A Man

There is a commercial for Capitol One credit that states, "What's in your wallet?" The question I am asking is, "What's on your mind?"

In the book of Matthew, chapter 15, the scribes and Pharisees asked Jesus why His disciples didn't wash their hands when they ate bread. Jesus answered by asking them why do they transgress the commandment of God by what they were doing. He also called them hypocrites (vs. 7) because they were saying one thing and doing another. There hearts were not right. Jesus also tells them that it is not what goes in the mouth that defiles a man but what comes out of him. Unless your doctor tells you not to eat pork because it will affect your health, it will not kill you.

It is the proper etiquette to wash your hands
before eating, but if you don't it will not harm
you. The most important thing is what you say
out of your mouth. The Bible also reads that evil
thoughts, murders, adulteries, fornications, thefts,
false witness and blasphemies are the things that
defile a man, not eating food without washing
your hands (vs. 19, 20). What's on your mind?
We also know that if you smoke cigarettes, drink
alcohol and do drugs that these things will also
kill you. When we eat, the food goes into the
belly and exits when we use the bathroom. But
when evil words come out of your mouth, it
comes from the heart.

Matthew 15:15-17 reads, "Peter answered and
said unto him, Declare unto us this parable." And
Jesus said, "Are ye also yet without
understanding? Do not ye yet understand, that
whatsoever entereth in at the mouth goeth into the
belly and is cast out into the drought?" All the
acid that is in your stomach is going to dissolve
the food that you put in it. That is why you

shouldn't chew gum on an empty stomach. All the acid that is in your stomach will make you sick. The only thing that food is going to do is make you overweight.

Ephesians 4:29 says, "Let no corrupt communication proceed out of your mouth, but that which is good to the use of edifying, that it may minister grace unto the hearers." Get away from people who want to talk dirty about men and women. You have no right to comment on someone who is not your husband or wife. Some of us have been in conversations like that in the church. That is wicked. When you let your mind be wicked, you grieve God and the Holy Ghost.

In Proverbs 29:1 it reads, "He being often reproved hardened his neck, shall be suddenly destroyed, and that without remedy." If someone has to keep on correcting you, you are not very smart. If someone has to keep telling you something over and over again, something is wrong with your head. You harden your neck and say, "I do what I want to do and say what I want to say and nobody is going to stop me. I put on my pants just like he does."

One of the prelay bishops of the P.C. of A.F., Bishop Dr. D. Rayford Bell, always says, "You don't know how I put on my pants. I might put them on the wall and jump in them."

The aforementioned scripture reminds us that continual reproving stiffens your neck. God will literally take you out of here. There will be no cure for whatever disease or sickness is ailing you. He will hit you with a seed of cancer. There once was a woman who used to stand in front of the church just to smoke her cigarettes. The church members would always try to get her to come in to the services but she would often tell them, "I am not coming in that old church." For some unknown reason, she hardened her heart and stiffened her neck. A few months later she was stricken with cancer and died. There was no cure for her. There was also a sister that attended our church and was corrected about the way she had been dressing after being in church a while. After so long, you shouldn't come to church dressed like you are walking the streets. She said she would never come back to church again. A few months later she was killed instantly. You have to watch what you say and who you say it to. You have to watch what you say because you just might get what you ask for. You just might not make it back.

The Bible tells us to let no corrupt communication come out of our mouths. No means no. The Bible also tells us to guard our heart, for out of it comes the issues of life. We need to guard our heart with all diligence. Grieve not the Holy Spirit. Stop letting things just come out of your mouth. Don't let things jump out of your mouth like a leap frog.

You have to deal with yourself. You can't say evil things. Put those things away and stop tripping. You have to say, "I am a child of God. I am not going to say those things and I am not going to think like that." Those are the devils words and thoughts. The devil wants you to say things to hurt people. You go on the job blasting your co-workers out. You almost curse your boss out. The Bible tells us that we can't bring forth bitter and sweet water at the same time. You curse, swear and lie out of one side of your mouth and bless the Lord out of the other side.

Psalms 5:7-9 says, "But as for me, I will come into thy house in the multitude of thy mercy: and in fear will I worship toward thy holy temple. Lead me, O Lord, in thy righteousness because of mine enemies; make thy way straight before my face. For there is no faithfulness in their mouth; their inward part is very wickedness; their throat is an open sepulcher; they flatter with their tongue." People say things and don't mean it. People throw things in the air and don't mean them. People throw things in the air and don't mean them. It is best not to say anything, just do it. Their throats are open graves. They love to say what they are going to do and how they are going to do it. They have no steadfastness or faithfulness. Stick to the plan. People like to throw you off the plan.

James 3:5-18 tells us, "Even so the tongue is a little member, and boasteth great things, behold, how great a matter a little fire kindleth! And the tongue is a fire, a world of iniquity: so is the tongue among our member, that it defileth the whole body, and setteth on fire the course of nature; and it is set on fire of hell. For every kind of beasts, and of birds, and of serpents, and of things in the sea, is tamed, and hath been tamed of mankind; but the tongue can no man tame; it is an unruly evil, full of deadly poison. Therewith bless we God, even the Father; and therewith curse we men, which are made after the similitude of God. Out of the same mouth proceedeth blessing and cursing. My brethren, these things ought not so to be. Doth a fountain send forth at the same place sweet water and bitter? Can the fig tree, my brethren, bear olive berries? Either a vine figs? So can no fountain both yield salt water and fresh. Who is a wise and endued with knowledge among you? Let him shew out of a good conversation his works with meekness of wisdom. But if ye have bitter envying and strife in your hearts, glory not, and lie not against the truth. This wisdom descendeth not from above, but is earthly, sensual and devilish. For where envying and strife is, there is confusion and every evil work. But the wisdom that is from above is first pure, then peaceable, gentle, and easily to be intreated, full of mercy and good fruits without partiality, and without hypocrisy. And the fruit of righteousness is sown in peace of them that make peace."

All it takes is a little spark to burn down a whole building in a matter of minutes. There is a whole lot if iniquity in our tongues. We need to ask the Lord to bridle our tongues. The tongue, which is the smallest member, will defile the whole body. It will poison your spiritual and mental system. Why couldn't God speak through our toes or eyeballs? He had to save our tongue. He saved us through our tongue, or our glory, as King David calls it. The tongue is wicked. You can hurt people, slander their names

names and damage their credibility with your tongue. You can totally destroy someone by what you say. God can tame all of these things. Man can tame animals, birds and all types of creatures, but the tongue no man can tame. It is an unruly evil full of deadly poison. There is no cure for it but the Holy Ghost. The same people who sing dirty songs, curse, swear and degrade women are the ones on the award shows glorifying God for their dirty lyrics. Something is wrong. How are you going to say all of that crazy stuff and say that God gave you those lyrics? God did not give you that talent to use in that manner. The devil gives you those words when you write dirty songs. It is not God who gives you those filthy words to write. Those are earthly, sensual, (or natural) and devilish things. You ought not to be cursing. You can't have blessing and cursing coming out of your mouth. You can't say you are in the church and get with your friends and buddies and start cursing. You are not saved doing that mess. You need to stick your tongue in some blessed oil and tarry for the Holy Ghost again.

Proverbs 18:21 says, "Death and life are in the power of the tongue; and they that love it shall eat the fruit thereof." You have to watch what you say because in your tongue you can cause life or death. What you say can kill a person. It can destroy their influence and everything about them. Somebody can be thinking something good about a person and then look down on them because you are talking about them. The tongue is a little member that we can't control. Your mouth can be closed but inside your tongue is still moving. That is why we need the baptism of the Holy Ghost. God uses our tongue to allow us to speak in tongues.

The tongue is unruly and the Holy Ghost can tame it. You don't curse anymore. You don't say things out of the way. The only time you say things out of the way is when you override the Holy Ghost. Life and death are in the power of the tongue. What you say can affect somebody else. Anger, bitterness, malice, hatred, wrath, envy, jealousy, strife and conceit are in your heart that causes you to say things you shouldn't say.

You have to know when to say things. A person might be vulnerable at the time. They are not where they are supposed to be. They are on edge. It might be the right thing to say but not the right time to say it. Proverbs 25:11 says, "A word fitly spoken is like apples of gold in pictures of silver." If you are trying to put a square in a circle, it won't fit. You have to know when the opportune time is to say things. A lot of people commit suicide because people have said things to them at the wrong time. A man wanted to commit suicide when he came to one of our church services. After I preached the word of God he told me that it helped him. I don't know what I am going to say until God tells me what to say. I don't have sermons stored up for months. I ask God everyday, "Please give me something to say to your people." Whatever God has for the people is what I say. People have come to me after a service and said to me, "Pastor I needed to hear that today." They were wondering about certain things and situations and because I obeyed the voice of the Lord and said what He wanted me to say, and someone received it.

# Anger and Bitterness

The Bible tells us in Ephesians 4:26-27, "Be ye angry and sin not; let not the sun go down upon your wrath: neither give place to the devil." You are not supposed to be hitting anyone. Don't go to bed angry at your husband or wife. Get it straight before you close your eyes because you might not wake up in the morning. You don't know if you will wake up or go into eternity. The Bible doesn't tell us we can't get angry. If we are in the flesh we will get angry. There are going to be problems and situations that are going to upset us and get us all bent out of shape, but we cannot get angry and let the sun go down on our wrath. If we get to that place we are in bad shape. Don't give place to the devil so he can rear his ugly head in your house. Stop having a room prepared for the devil in your house.

Ephesians 4:31 reads, "Let all bitterness, and wrath, and anger, and clamour, and evil speaking,

be  put away from you, with all malice."  Get all
of the bitterness out of you heart.  People sit in the
church with deep seated bitterness.  Tell yourself,
"I am not going to get mad like this."  You have
to ask yourself, "Why am I getting mad like this
for no reason?"

The passage of scripture reads in Proverbs
29:8-23,  "Scornful men bring a city into a snare:
but wise men turn away wrath.  If a wise man
contended with a foolish man, whether he rage or
laugh, there is no rest.  The bloodthirsty hate the
upright: but the just seek his soul.  A fool uttereth
all his mind: but a wise man keepeth it in until
afterwards.  If a ruler hearken to lies, all his
servants are wicked.  The poor and the deceitful
man meet together: the Lord lightened both their
eyes.  The king that faithfully judgeth the poor,
his throne shall be established forever.  The rod
and reproof give wisdom: but a child left to
himself bringeth his mother to shame; when the
wicked are multiplied, transgression increaseth;
but the righteous shall see their fall.  Correct thy
son and he shall give thee rest; yea, he shall give

delight unto thy soul. Where there is no vision, the people perish: but he that keepeth the law, happy is he. A servant will not be corrected by words: for though he understand he will not answer. Seest thou a man hasty in his words? There is more hope of a fool than of him. He that delicately bringeth up his servant from a child shall have him become his son at the length. An angry man stirreth up strife, and a furious man aboundeth in transgression. A man's pride shall bring him low: but honor shall uphold the humble in spirit." A fool says everything that is on his mind. He can't keep anything. An angry man will stir up strife and get thing started and out of order because he is angry. A furious man abounds in trouble, or sin. If a man has a lot of foolish pride it will bring him down very low. But honor shall uphold a man with a humble spirit. He will have a lot of honor.

Going back to the book of Colossians, it tells us to set our affection on things above and not on things on the earth. It also tells us to mortify, or

kill out, the things that are in us. With this book I
will help you kill out the works of the mind. You
have to tell anger and bitterness, "I will kill you!"
I am tired of these things plaguing our people.
We have to be tired of the devil plaguing us.
Jesus said, through the lips of Paul, to the
Colossian church, "You have put off these things,
why do you keep on picking them up?" You have
to put off wrath, malice and anger. In this book I
will show you the difference.

Proverbs 28:13 reads, "He that covereth his
sins shall not prosper; but who confesseth and
forsaketh them shall have mercy." If you cover
things up you might as well confess and tell it and
get it out in the open so you can feel better. So
you can prosper. If don't open those things up
you will be miserable. You have to bring it out,
open it and lay it on the table. If you say, "Lord, I
don't want this anger or bitterness, please take this
out of my life," He will have mercy. You have to
want it out. We cannot have beautiful churches
with angry people. The devil brings anger, wrath
and bitterness because he doesn't want the church

to be happy. If the home is messed up the church is messed up. All the while, the pastor has to preach over messed up people.

In the word of God, Proverbs 14:10 says, "The heart knoweth his own bitterness; and a stranger doth not intermeddle with his joy." The devil also knows your bitterness because that is part of his attributes. He uses that against you. God knows the devils goods and that is why he wants to get it out of you.

Ecclesiastes 7:7-9 says, "Surely oppression maketh a wise man mad; and a gift destroyeth the heart. Better is the end of a thing than the beginning thereof: and the patient in spirit is better that the proud in spirit. Be not hasty in thy spirit to be angry; for anger resteth in the bosom of fools." Gifts soften the mind. You have to watch people giving gifts just so you won't preach on their sins. Don't be so anxious to do things. I used to be a very anxious person. I would buy cars and wouldn't need them. I wasn't patient at all.

If you are angry, the Bible calls you a fool. Anger takes residence in your spirit. It lies in your bosom. Don't be so quick to get angry. Think about what you are going to say. Ask yourself, "Would that damage their spirit if I said that? Will that give me gratification? Is this my payoff?" When you feel like you are getting angry, just inhale and exhale. Proverbs 16:32 says, "He that is slow to anger is better than the mighty; and he that ruleth his spirit than he that taketh a city." You are better than the mighty when you are slow to anger. You can see what is happening but you won't get mad. Do you have your spirit under control? People that are spirit led don't fly off the handle. It doesn't matter what people say, you still won't fly off the handle. Spirit led people listen to the spirit of God.

We are all in the same boat together. I am going to be honest and transparent. Some of us won't admit that we have problems in our lives with anger. I was once an angry man who married a sweet woman. I was saved but not delivered. You might ask, "How can that happen?" It happens everyday. I was not delivered from my anger or bitterness. I was preaching, teaching, singing and helping my pastor with my anger. I would come home stressed out and take it out on my wife. I never laid a hand on her but sometimes what we say can do even more damage. Physical wounds heal but emotional and mental scars last forever. Some people are saved but not delivered. I heard fussing and arguing growing up and I started doing it. It got to a point where my wife would just stop talking and start crying. I would say thing I wish would have never come out of my mouth. I didn't call her names or anything. I would just say hurtful things and she would just cry. Don't have your wife crying all the time for nothing. I would ask her what she was crying for, but I just wounded her by what I just said. We say things that hurt one another. We say things because we are angry and bitter at someone else. I was angry with my father and my broken home and took it out on my wife. She was in the same situation but she didn't take it our on me. Her father once hit her mother in the face with a bat.

She saw things just like I did. She could have been abusive to me. What she saw could have been imbedded in her and destroyed her life. What you see can get in your spirit. If you say, "I am not going to be like that" then that is the way you end up. One thing I said when I was fourteen years old was that I would never take my money and throw it away like my father did. I would never leave my kids like my father did so often. I also said that my father didn't teach me anything. The Holy Ghost told me that he did. He taught me how to take care of my wife and children because it was something that he did not do. Some other aspects of my childhood slipped over into my marriage without my knowledge. I was angry with my wife without a cause. I was fussing and didn't know why. My wife would just sit there crying because of something I said.

There are not only angry men but also angry women. There are people who are mad at the world because they got dealt a bad hand. There are different types of bitterness. Everybody is not bitter about the same thing.

Put off anger, wrath, malice, blasphemy and filthy communication. Put off anger. Stop wearing the coat of anger. Take the coat off and throw it away. Put off getting so mad that you want to tear something up. You have to put off the old man. Do you have the old man off yet? Some of us are still carrying the old, dead man around. In the old days, if you murder a man in cold blood your punishment would be to have that person strapped on your back until it rotted on you. The apostle Paul said, "Who shall deliver me from the body of this death?" Sin is like a dead man on your back. Put on the new man. The new man is life. He is alive and fresh. The old man stinks with anger, bitterness, malice, wrath, hatred, envy, jealousy, strife and conceit. The devil tries to get us angry through family members. He tried to get anger stirred up in me so I wouldn't be able to teach Bible class and write this book.

Jesus comes first before anybody. If He is not going to be first, He is not going to be anything. Jesus told John, "I am Alpha and Omega, the beginning and the end." God is everything in between.  If you have someone that you love more than God, then they are your God.  Do you have on the new man?  You will be surprised by how many people in the church don't have on the new man. God created you so you should wear Him.

Matthew 5:22 tells us not to be angry with our brothers without a cause.  We have to be careful about calling our brothers and sisters empty headed fools.  If we do then we are in danger of hell fire.  A rock group had a song titled, "There's A Fire Down Below" and "Highway to Hell." Matthew 5:23 tells us we need to get ourselves right and our minds clear.  A tub represents washing.  We must wash ourselves by the water and the Word.  We need to keep ourselves washed.  After we have washed ourselves we need to clean our tubs so someone else can use it.

Luke 15:27-32 is the end of the story of the prodigal son.  The other son got angry because his father threw a party for the son that went away. Why would you get angry when God does something for someone else?  You should be happy for your brother and sister in the Lord. There are people who are upset with me because I am blessed. If your brother is gone for so long and he makes up his mind to return to God you would think that he would be accepted with open arms. You would think saints would be happy when sinners and backsliders come to the Lord. You would think they would put their arms around them and say, "God loves you and I do too." The brother, in the story of the prodigal son, was angry because the father showed kindness and compassion to his sibling. Because he was gone for a long time doesn't make him any less of a son than the other. I don't care where my sons are, they are still mine. Bad or good, sons or daughters, they are still my children. That is way God looks at it. You can be a backslidden son but you are still His child. He may me mad or disappointed in you but you are still His.

The father threw the former wayward son a party. People don't want to throw a party when sinners come back to the Lord. The father in this story represents God. Everybody is not going to be happy when God blesses you. "How is God going to do that for her and she just got back in the church?" Who are you working for? What is your motive? Are you in the church just for the fish and the loaves? We complain and say, "Look at what I am doing, I have been here for a long time." I am writing this book to tell you to keep on doing what you are doing and God will bless you. In the story the other son referred to his brother as "thy son." People will disclaim you when they get upset. Because he is upset with him he is not his brother but rather "thy son." The father told him that he will always have what he has. You don't have to be jealous of anyone because you are already in the church. You should be glad when people get themselves together. Why are you so angry and judgmental? What's on your mind? Why are you so green with envy? You are just angry for no reason. We have to watch the way we think when people come back to the church. What kind of prayers are we praying? Are we praying that people get saved or are we praying that they stay out there in the world? We need to cry with tears on the altar for our brother and sisters to come back to the Lord and get saved. They could die out there in the world without God.

Your mind has to be right in the sight of God. Matthew 8:18-23 reads that Simon saw the Holy Ghost being given and thought he had to pay for it but Peter rebuked him and him that his heart was not right. If you are doing something other than the right thing then your mind is messed up. You have the wrong intentions. What's on your mind? We need to repent and turn from the ways we are thinking. Peter understood that Simon was bitter. People who are bitter might as well be into witchcraft and devil worshipping. They are angry with someone. People who are into drugs are angry with someone. Drugs are a spirit. When you get hooked on drugs you start stealing, selling your body and doing things that you wouldn't normally do. You are bitter about something that happened in your life. It didn't start in your adulthood. It started in your childhood.

Have you ever tasted something bitter in your mouth?  Some people are like that.  Everyone they come in contact with, they try to make bitter. When people get bitter they start doing a whole lot of crazy things.  You did wild things and no one could tame you.  You did other things to try to cover it up but you couldn't because you were bitter.  There are some people who have poison on their tongue.  They can poison your spirit with their bitterness.  They can make you bitter even when bitterness was not present in your spirit.  I can never emphasize enough that it started in your childhood.  It's like a snake bit when you were a child and you were poisoned with its venom.  You started looking for love in all the wrong places because you have the devils venom in you.  It's in your vein.  The only way you can get it out of you is if you go down in the name of Jesus and let Him wash and cleanse you and give you a spiritual blood transfusion.  Romans 3:13-18 talks about the bitter person whose mouth is full of cursing and like an open sepulcher or graveyard. People who are bitter and miserable are very swift to do crazy things.  There is an old saying that states, "misery loves company." If they don't praise God then they don't want you to. I would be on the job singing and praising God and my coworkers would start things with me. There was a coworker who always wanted to fight. He was a bitter man. There are different types of bitterness that people house in their spirit.

We should be fruit inspectors. If you say you are an apple or peach tree, then apples and peaches should be growing on your tree, not lemons. Lemons are the works of the flesh. The fruits of the spirit are synonymous to apples, peaches, pears and plums, nice and sweet. Sweet things should be on your tree. When I buy fruit, I like it to be sweet if that is the way it is supposed to taste. When you get a sweet watermelon you can eat yourself crazy. The works of the flesh are like garlic and leeks. You don't want bitter stuff. God eradicated all bitter stuff when He died on the cross. We should no longer live with the works of the flesh in our bodies.

Proverbs 22:24-29 says, "Make no friendship
with an angry man; and with a furious man thou
shalt not go: lest thou learn his ways, and get a
snare to thy soul. Be not thou one of them that
strike hands, or of them that are sureties for debts.
If thou has nothing to pay, why should he take
away thy bed from under thee? Remove not the
ancient landmark, which thy fathers have set.
Seest thou a man diligent in his business? He
shall not stand before mean men." You cannot
get with angry people. They have bad attitudes
that will rub off on you. Have you ever been
around people talking crazy and they get you
stirred up back out on you. The Bible tells us that
evil communication corrupt good manner. You
can be the best person in the world, but if you get
around people with negative attitudes and
negative thoughts you will be negative. All of the
negativity that is in them will rub off on you.
There is a saying, "birds of a feather flock
together." If you stay around mad people all the
time, you will be mad. People will see that you
are not the same anymore until you started
hanging around that person. Don't have the desire

to be with an angry man. A furious man is super mad. He is envious, full of wrath, angry, bitter and full of strife. Unless you learn what he is doing, you will start acting like he does. You will mess up you own soul acting like angry people.

Jonah got upset with God because He did not destroy Nineveh. Jonah 4:1 reads, "But it displeased Jonah exceedingly, and he was very angry." God said he would destroy Nineveh but they turned around and repented. People will get mad because you make a turn around and want to live for the Lord. While praying to God, Jonah was also mad at Him. How can you get down on your knees, that God made, and pray to Him with madness and anger in your heart? Jonah told God, "I knew you weren't going to destroy this country." People don't like to be good to bad people. They will get mad if you try to do something nice for someone who is not so nice. If you have the love of God in your heart you will do something good for somebody even if they treat you bad.

Jonah ran from what God wanted him to do. He knew that God would change His mind about destroying Nineveh. How many times have we done the opposite of what God told us to do because we knew the end result would be something good for that person? Job knew that God would have mercy on Nineveh so he went the other way. He didn't realize that he was the instrument to getting Nineveh some mercy. Just like the story of the prodigal son that closes out with his brother on the outside angry because his brother cam back to his father's house. Don't think people are happy when you come back to church to return for good. They should but don't think they will be. They don't like it when you are restored to the place where you left. What they don't know is when you went and got everything straight and repented. A lot of people will miss heaven because they see the end result and not what happened before you got back. I don't mess with anything God does. If a man repents, what can you or anyone else do about it? If he didn't blaspheme against God, he can be saved. You can't do anything with a man that repents. I don't care what he has done. There is no preacher, bishop, minister or anyone else that can do anything about it.  God is the one who gives the final say on where you are going.  There was a man who said that we shoot our wounded.  There are people who are wounded and we are still shooting them.  We are supposed to mend them up and pour oil in their wounds to get them back in shape to start fighting the devil again.  We are not to say, "What are they doing here?  They should have stayed out there."  What kind of spirit do you have?  Peter asked God to rain down fire on the people just like Elijah did. You are not supposed to talk like that if you are saved. You are supposed to have mercy on people.  The Bible tells us to, "Take heed to yourselves, lest ye fall." You will need mercy one day and you will not get it because you did not give any.  I don't want God to say He doesn't have any mercy for me because I didn't have any mercy for anyone else.  Jonah told God that he knew He was merciful.  God is slow to anger.  He is not quick to kill anyone.  God changed His mind about what He would do to Jonah.  Furthermore, God can't repent because we can't accuse Him of anything.  Jonah got so mad that he asked God to kill him because he thought that God had made a fool of him. Jonah wanted to die because he preached to Nineveh and told them that God would kill them and He didn't. History gives an account that some of Jonah's uncles went to Nineveh and preached and they killed them, cut their head off and hung them before the sun with their genitals in their mouths. That is why Jonah was angry with God; because he did not destroy Nineveh for what they did to his family. We shouldn't be mad because momma or daddy is mad. We don't even know what went on to cause them to be angry. God knew that Jonah was angry. Jonah was still waiting to see if God was going to destroy the city. Jonah had pity on the gourd that God placed on him but not on the people of Nineveh.

If people are angry, just pray for them. Judges 18:25-27 says, "And the children of Dan said unto him, Let not thy voice be heard among us, lest angry fellow run upon thee, and thou lose thy life, with the loves of thy household." Don't stay around angry people when they are mad. It will do no good.  You cannot reason with an angry man.  If he is mad, he can't hear anything.  Some people get so mad they have blood in their eyes.  Their veins pop out of their heads.  You cannot reason with them.

In Samuel, chapter 1, verse 10, Hannah was bitter because she was barren and didn't have any children.  She wanted a child and God blessed her with Samuel.  Sometimes things happen in our lives that make us bitter.  When people are bitter they cry and complain all the time.  They find fault with other people and nothing is ever right.  You will find yourself at your own pity party when you are bitter.  If you are always around bitter and distressed people that spirit will jump on you and you will be the same way.  1st Samuel 22:2 reads, "And everyone that was in distress, and everyone that was in debt, and everyone that was discontented, gathered themselves unto him; and he became a captain over them; and there were with him about four hundred men."

In 2$^{nd}$ Kings, chapter 4, verse 20, the man of God knew what was wrong with the woman but his assistant pushed her away. The woman was vexed. The word vexed means bitter. Some women are bitter because of things that happened in their lives. Some thing you have to do different. You have to have a different method and approach. When the prophet Elijah came, he came with a different method. The woman's child was dead for days but the man of God laid upon him and the child sneezed seven times and was alive again. The same man of God that told her she would have a child restored so that the root of bitterness would come out of her. God sees our afflictions and know that we get bitter sometimes. He knows what we are going through and how we feel. In 2$^{nd}$ Samuel 14, God knew the affliction of Israel. He knew they were bitter. God knows we are bitter but he wants us to get rid of it. The devil is the author of confusion. He confuses matters and has us bitter towards one another. God doesn't want His church like that. He doesn't want families, children, husbands and wives like that.

It is bad business when you are bitter and envious. Don't be bitter and envious and full of strife. Don't glorify bitter, strife and envying in your heart. Don't glorify things like that because it is of the devil and not of God. There is confusion where people are envious, have strife and are mad and hate one another and there is also every evil work when there are these works of the flesh evident in your spirit. People with these things in their spirit are not quiet. There is a bunch of confusion. God's spirit is infusible and peaceable. If you make peace you have the fruit of righteousness. There is so much trouble in the Middle East because they have fake treaties. Don't make trouble, make peace. They make you think they have peace and the next thing you know they are strapping themselves with bombs and blowing up innocent people. Saints should make peace with one another. You cannot be saved and not make peace. If you are housing bitterness, envy and strife in your heart, you cannot be saved.

In Psalms 64:3-7, God is not talking about a natural sword but He is talking about the tongue. People can say bitter things to you. They can cut you in half and rip your heart out. They can shoot in secret at the perfect. They will try to knock you out of the box.

There are people who are so bitter and nasty, they throw rocks and hide their hands. When you confront them, they deny it. They are the main ones shooting arrows. They put on a front. They look so innocent and say it wasn't them. They do it suddenly and without fear. They don't fear talking about the man of God. They encourage themselves about doing wrong. They hurt people and think that they are alright. They are envious so they lay snares for the righteous. They plot against the ones who are living right. They tell people who don't know you, mean and hurtful things about you to ruin your character.

It is time for us to stop snoring and sleeping and be heavenly minded and be more spiritual about God's business. If we get more into God, all envy, anger, bitterness, malice, strife, hatred, jealousy and conceit, he will kill it. Wake up out of your sleep! Do you know that Jesus is now closer to His coming than when our forefathers were here? Why are we still tripping? Jesus will catch people unawares with these things still in them. We are still hating, envying and having strife. Some people have murder in their hearts. Don't be like you were when you were in the world. You did crazy things. Cast off the works of darkness. The devil doesn't want you to prosper and God to bless you. He wants you to wear the coat of darkness. Cast it off! Just take it and pull it off. That is not what you are supposed to be wearing. Cast off the works of the devil. Put on the armour of light. Be honest in your dealing with people. You shouldn't be crooked and slick in the church. You shouldn't be cutting and undermining people in the church. Those are the works of darkness. You shouldn't be hateful and deceitful in the church. Not in rioting and being drunk.

You can be drunk with anger. You can be drunk with the works of the flesh. When you have all of these things you are intoxicated with the devils' liquor. When a man is intoxicated he can't be reasoned with. When people get in a rage you can't talk to them. They are so angry blood gets in their eyes. You can't be full of anger, strife or envy. You have to put on the Lord Jesus Christ.

A whole lot of people will get messed up because you are bitter. Don't get bitter. The root will not only trouble other people but it will mess your mind and heart up. Bitterness will make you sell out against God. You will do something God didn't tell you to do. Esau was crying bitterly with tears but there was no mercy. When you get bitter you will sell your birthright. The right to be saved, holy and sanctified.

God doesn't get mad or angry like we do. We get mad at the drop of a hat. Some of us won't admit it, but we are some of the most angry people in the world. The Bible says, "Come, let us reason together. God even tells us to reason.

You can't reason with an angry man. He won't even feel you pulling on him. I have been that mad before. I am being real. I have been so mad that I couldn't hear anybody. I couldn't feel anyone pulling on me. I thank God I don't get that mad anymore. The devil tried to get me but I didn't make that appointment. The devil knows how I like things so he tries to mess my whole day up. God is slow to anger. You have to do real crazy things for God to get upset.

There are a lot of angry people in the world. Judges 18:25 says, "And the children of Dan said unto him, Let not thy voice be heard among us, lest angry fellows run upon thee, and thou lose thy life, with the lives of thy household." There are murdering demons in this world. A man once murdered his mother in law, wife and children. When that murdering demon jumps off of him he won't know why he did it. This is a very angry world. Everybody is just angry and upset. It silently creeps into the church. We are all perplexed and confused about certain things. There used to be a time when we were so joyful.

Now we are so angry. When we didn't have anything we were happy. Now that we have things and get them when we want them we are even more confused and perplexed.

In the book of Esther, chapter 4, Mordecai was angry. He cried with a loud and bitter cry. He was very angry. It is not good to be angry. Anger raises your blood pressure and causes complications in your body. Esther 4:1-2 says, "When Mordecai perceived all that was done, Mordecai rent his clothes, and put on sackcloth with ashes, and went out into the midst of the city, and cried with a loud and bitter cry, and came even before the kings gate: for none might enter into the king's gate clothed with sackcloth.

Job is another great example of anger. Job 13:26 says, "For thou writest bitter things against me to possess the iniquities of my youth." He even cursed the day that he was born. Some people wish they were never born because of the bad and evil things that happened to them in their childhood. You can smile, shout and dance over it but you are still angry because nobody was there to protect and help you. Job 3:1-5, 20 reads, "After this opened Job his mouth, and cursed his day. And Job spake and said, Let the day perish wherein I was born, and the night in which it was said, There is a man child conceived. Let that day be darkness, let not God regard if from above, neither let the light shine upon it. Let darkness and the shadow of death stain it; let the blackness of the day terrify it. Wherefore is the light given to him that is in misery, and life unto the bitter in soul." Job had a very bitter soul. People who are angry are bitter.

Jeremiah 20:18 says, "Wherefore I came forth out of the womb to see labour and sorrow, that my days should be consumed with shame?" It all comes from your youth. It does not come from your adulthood. Everything you are dealing with now, even your personality, comes from your youth. How you act was picked up from someone you were influenced by. Everybody has scars. Scars that cannot be seen. Scars that have been covered by hairstyles, clothes, purses, shoes, choir and ministers robes and even a shout and a dance. These scars are not visible. They make us bitter because we've never had any closure. Before the end of this book we are going to get closure. You are going to heal in Jesus' name!

Job's complaint was bitter. We sometimes have bitter complaints with nothing good to say. Job was trying to find the Lord so he could complain and argue with him. Have you ever argued with God? We try to act like we don't but we do. Not like arguing with your husband or wife but just complaining about finances, body aches and everything else. Job 23:1-17 reads, "Then Job answered and said, Even today is my complaint bitter: my stroke is heavier than my groaning. Oh that I knew where I might find him! That I might come even to his seat! I would order my cause before him, and fill my mouth with arguments. I would know the words which he would answer me, and understand what he would say to me. There the righteous might dispute with him; so should I be delivered for ever from my judge. Behold, I go forward, but he is not there;

and backward, but I cannot perceive him: on the left hand, where he doth work, but I cannot behold him: he hideth himself on the right hand, that I cannot see him: but he knoweth the way that I take: when he hath tried me, I shall come forth as gold. My foot hath held his steps, his way have I kept, and not declined. Neither have I gone back from the commandment of his lips; I have esteemed the words of his mouth more than my necessary food. But he is in one mind, and who can turn him? And what is soul desireth, even that he doeth. For he performeth the thing that is appointed for me: and many such things are with him. Therefore am I troubled at his presence: when I consider, I am afraid of him. For God maketh my heart soft and the Almighty troubleth me; because I was not cut off before the darkness, neither hath he covered the darkness from my face."

Job 27:1-10 reads, "Moreover Job continues this parable, and said, As God liveth, who hath taken away my judgment; and the Almighty, who hath vexed my soul; all the while my breath is in me, and the spirit of God is in my nostrils; my lips shall not speak wickedness; my tongue utter deceit. God forbid that I should justify you: till I die I will not remove mine integrity from me. My righteousness I hold fast, and will not let it go: my heart shall not reproach me so long as I live. Let mine enemy be as the wicked, and he that riseth up against me as the unrighteous. For what is the hope of the hypocrite, thou he hath gained, when God taketh away his soul? Will God hear his cry when trouble cometh upon him? Will he delight himself in the Almighty? Will he always call upon God?" You have to watch being slick with your tongue. Bitterness will make you a slick person. Because somebody hurt you, you want to hurt someone else. People who are bitter are cunning and sly. They do things undercover. They will smile in your face and be cutting you all along. Deceitful people are bitter. They are in the church and in the world. They speak in tongues and dance with you. They are working with you and me. They will say something to hurt them so they can hurt somebody. Don't think that it is not happening in the church today. They won't even leave the church. They will stay right in the house of God and be a thorn in somebody's flesh. They out shout you and everybody else. You have to be able to mark a deceitful person.

Some people will keep blaming and accusing other people of things, that all the blaming they are doing will blame themselves right in hell because they are not taking care of number one. They are not making sure that number one is right. All of the bickering, arguing, fussing and fighting that people are doing will send them straight to hell because they just won't leave it alone. You have to leave things alone. It will cause you to miss out on heaven. It is not worth it. It is best to stay quiet and say nothing. People will have your soul bitter. A preacher called me and tried to feel me out. He tried to find out where I stand. He tried to put something in my heart. I know how to get them straight in a nice way. When you want to get your point across you don't have to be mean and you don't have to holler or scream.

Whenever you hear the word woe, it is not good. When God says woe it is not good. Isaiah 5:20, 21 reads, "Woe unto them that call evil, good and good, evil; that put darkness or light and light for darkness; that put bitter for sweet and sweet for bitter! Woe into them that are wise in their own eyes, and prudent in their own sight!" Some people think that darkness is better than light. Watch out thinking you all that and you know it all. You act like nobody can tell you anything. You won't take anyone's advice. You think you are already up there. Some people mix strong drinks together and get as drunk as they can. You didn't think the Bible talked about that did you? Bitter people go get drunk. They are mad about something that happened in your childhood so they drink to ground their sorrows thinking that is the only way to get rid of them. They become alcoholics, causing them to beat their wives and children. They rape their daughters or sons. This is what happens when you let the works of the flesh control you. The Bible has an answer for everything that life has to offer.

Some people don't want to be comforted because they are bitter. Bitterness is a comfort zone for some people. They feel good when they are bitter. They are very vengeful. They like to get back at people. People are like that in the church of the living God. They are in your midst. They shout, preach, teach, sing, usher, they are on the deacon board and in the music and audio ministry. They are everywhere. You can't detect them. You don't know who they are because they smile every time they see you. They say, "Praise the Lord" just like you do. They raise their hands and magnify God just like you do. The preacher tells them to shake three peoples hand and they shake six. They want to let you know that they are spiritual. They cover it up with a lot of hugging and kissing. They hate your guts. They would pull your heart out if they could. They can't stand you more than they can stand a possum running across them in the street. They sing like angels and preach like Paul. We don't think that it is in our churches but it is.

It is a bitter and evil thing to forsake God. It is bad when you have no fear of God. You are in bad shape when you can't fear God. Jeremiah 2:19-21 says, "Thine own wickedness shall correct thee, and thy backslidings shall reprove thee: know therefore and see that it is an evil thing and bitter, that thou hast forsaken the Lord thy God and that my fear is not in thee, saith the Lord God of host. For of old time I have broken thy yoke, and burst thy bands; and thou sadist, I will not transgress; when upon every high hill and under every green tree thou wanderest, playing the harlot. Yet I had planted thee a noble vine, wholly a right seed: how then art thou turned into the degenerate plant of a strange vine unto me?

Anytime people do wicked things they have a seed of bitterness that has been planted in them. It is not a sweet thing anytime you try to hurt people. Jeremiah 4:18 says, "Thy way and thy doing have procured these things unto thee; this is thy wickedness, because it is bitter, because it reacheth into thine heart." You try to say things to hurt people. You might say, "I didn't mean to say that." Yes you did. The Bible tells us that out of the abundance of the heart the mouth speaks. What is in your heart is going to come out of your mouth. Jesus knew what was on His disciples' mind. He perceived their thoughts. He asked them, "Why are you reasoning within your hearts?" I know what's on your mind. Anger, jealousy, conceit, wrath, bitterness, malice, strife and envy are on your mind. These things go into your heart. That is why you have to be careful how you hear and what you hear. I don't care if it is your mother. If your mother isn't talking right you have to tell her that you can't hear it. If she is talking about the church, pastor and first lady you have to walk out. Don't stand there and listen to it. If you stay it will affect you. Don't listen to snake talk. Anybody who is talking about your church and running it down is not right and is getting it straight from the devil. Eve listened to the devil and he wiled away her time. When your resistance is down you can't fight effectively.

While training for a fight, a trainer has to build up his/her resistance. He has to train and run a few miles a day. He has to stay in shape because his opponent is doing the same thing that he is. He can't go running the streets and drinking. He has to train six months in advance and sometimes longer. He can't be sexually intimate with his wife for six months. His opponent is ranked number one. He can't be out there eating a whole lot of hamburgers and stuff that is not going to make him fit and trim for the fight. He will get knocked out. You can't run in the ring thinking you have the advantage because you are the champion. You have to stay in shape.

The devil wore Eve out to the point where she thought she was going to die. He got her to question God. The devil will get you to question God if you start listening to him. He told Eve to eat from the tree and God wasn't going to do anything. They found out that God was not playing. God found out and asked them who told then they were naked. He asked the devil if he had any part in it.

Don't get around people who are downsizing their brother and sister. Get away from them. Stay away from people with nasty attitudes. They are bitter. If they are always running you and everybody else down, get away from them. They will tell you, "Girl, I was just playing." No they weren't playing, they meant what they said. If it was something to tear your character down, they meant it. They tried to hurt you and laugh over it. They will mess your mind up and have you looking at other people and the next thing you know you will be leaving the church. You will leave and nobody has done anything to you. The pastor doesn't even know what is going on. People just walk out the church and don't know what they are mad about. They will put a root of bitterness in you and you don't even know why. They will do it because they are bitter. Stay away from people who talk all the time. Don't have any part with those kinds of people. I don't care if they sing in the choir with you. The Bible tells us to mark the people who cause division.

Another scripture tells us to have no fellowship with them. Love them and keep on walking. They will make your spirit bitter if you stay around them long enough. They will mess you up. When you first came into the church everybody was saved until the bitter person got to you. Everybody was saved and going to heaven until that bitter person started pointing out and naming people. You thought they were the sweetest people on earth until the bitter person started dogging them. Because you just came into the church, you don't know any better. All you see are sweet and sanctified people. All you see are loving people.

People can make your mind wicked and corrupt because they haven't gotten rid of the works of the mind. They never accepted the chance to get their mind renewed. They never got their spirit renewed. They still have the same old mind they had when they were in the world. Saints are not supposed to have that type of mind. They still have that type of mind because they didn't get delivered. They wouldn't let God

change their mind.  The Bible tells us to let the
mind that is in Christ Jesus be our mind.  You
have to let God's mind be in you.  You have to
start thinking and talking like Jesus.  Your
mannerism has to be like his.  People are still
cursing because their minds haven't changed.
They won't let the Holy Ghost convict them.
When the Holy Ghost convicts you, you will want
to change your mind.  You will ask the Lord to
forgive you if your mind has changed.  If you
really want to change you will ask the Lord to
help you.  The devil is a liar.  Those thoughts
don't come from God, they come from the devil.
It is not originated from God.  Those things are
sinful, devilish and hellish.  The devil doesn't
want you to identify the works of the flesh.  Just
because your mother was an Indian doesn't mean
that you have to be mean.  We want to blame
things on our grandparents but they are dead now.
God saved you.  He wants to renew your mind but
every time He tries to you shut him out.  You
close your ears.  That is why Jesus said, "He that
hath an ear, let him hear what the spirit is saying
to the church."  If you don't hear what God is

saying, you will do something crazy. The devil will plant those things in your mind and make you think that they are alright. The devil cares nothing about you. Why would you hear your pastor preach and teach and go out the same way that you came in? You should get in your prayer closet and ask God to help you. Nobody has to know that you have issues. God knows and He is the only one that can help you. You have to get it corrected, if you don't all those things that you are dealing with will surface.

An alcoholic's skin starts to stink because he drinks all the time. The stench of the alcohol starts to come through his pores. That is how the works of the mind are. If you let those things stay in you for a long time they will start to come out. You can smile over it for so long that if someone rubs you the wrong way it is coming out. You might say that you are saved and that fighting spirit is gone but if someone plucks that last nerve you will soon find out that it is not as far gone as you thought it was. You will feel like knocking somebody's head off. You will feel like you did before you got saved. You will even sometimes feel like killing someone. Everyone is capable of murder whether it is on accident or on purpose. A man dead on accident is as dead as a man that is dead on purpose. These things are the works of the mind that activate the works of the flesh. If it is in your mind you will fulfill it in your flesh. If you think about something long enough you will do it. When a bank is robbed it is first cased by the perpetrator(s). When I was a little boy some guys cased my house for a few days. They knew when we left and what time we came back. After they found out how to get in they robbed our home. If you were a thief before you were saved the devil may try to tempt you to steal from the church. He doesn't tempt you with things that you have never done. If you are not spiritually and mentally up with God the devil will mess with you. He will mess with you with old boyfriends and girlfriends. That fire has been out, but he will try to rekindle it. He will strike the match until it flames up. You're looking at him, she is looking at you. That relationship has been over. It is dead. The devil will get you to start thinking about how it used to be. You should turn to him and say, "God don't need no matches, he's fire all by himself." Jeremiah said, "It's like fire shut up in my bones!"

I was driving along in my Suburban minding my own business and I looked over at the car across from me and the woman tried to give me the eye. I didn't know who they were so I just sped away. I already have my sweetheart. She has been my sweetheart for 30 years. I am not playing games. If you sit there long enough things will happen. Anything that is in your mind (don't think you are too old, just asked Abraham) to do you will do it. Sin knows no age. An eighty-eight-year-old man and an eighty year old woman had to get sat down for committing adultery. There is no age limit. I know they didn't have Viagra back then. Whatever you do goes into your heart. The Bible tells us to guard our heart. We need to guard our heart because out of it comes the issues of life. You have to guard your heart and your mind. The devil will mess with your heart and mind. We have to stay prayerful and keep the works of the mind out of our hearts. He will create bitterness and your heart. You don't want to be a bitter person.

Don't be bitter against your brother or your sister. Be mad at the devil. He is still your enemy. Your husband, wife or children are not your enemies. It is the devil. Don't take your bitterness out on your children. Some people don't want to be comforted when they are bitter. They want to be left allow and don't want anybody to comfort them. Jeremiah 31: 15 says, "The saith the Lord; a voice was heard in Ramah, lamentation, and bitter weeping: Rachel weeping for her children refused to be comforted for her children, because they were not." I once hugged somebody's child and the father came to me and said, "Don't you touch my child." Adam rose up in me. I had a water hose in my hand that had water in it that got to 250°. I was not always as saved as I am now. I told him that his child was going to be warped just like he was. I know I should not have said that. Sometimes we say things we shouldn't say. By the way I was feeling

I was going to burn him with that water. I wasn't
going to let him hurt me. That was the end of this
now. I still have some work to do on my flesh.
And so do you. Your flesh is not all gone. Your
flesh is not saved. Your inner man gives saved.
If your flesh is not controlled by the Spirit, it will
act up. Especially if you have been feeding off of
anger all of your life your flesh will rise up. You
will feel it all over your face. I have felt anger so
heavy that I have felt heat in my chest. My face
got hot and my eyes got red. Your blood pressure
goes up. You can't feel anybody pulling on you.
The Bible tells of the anger rests in the bosom of a
fool. If I get angry a few minutes later, I can
forget all about it. You can't hold on to that stuff.
It rottens your bones. The Bible tells us that your
bones will ache because of bitterness. You don't
want to be like that. Saints are supposed to be
sweet. Everything you come in contact with will
have honey on it because you're so sweet. You
have a sweet attitude. What's on your mind?

Ezekiel 3: 14 says, "So the spirit lifted me up,
and took me away, and I went in bitterness, in the

heat of my spirit; but the hand Lord was strong upon me." Ezekiel 27: 30, 31 reads, "And shall cause their voice to be heard against thee, and they shall cry bitterly, and shall cast up dust upon their heads, they shall wallow themselves in the ashes: and they shall make themselves utterly bald for thee, and gird them with sackcloth, and they shall weep for thee with bitterness of heart and bitter wailing." Ruth 1: 20 -22, "And she said unto them, call me not Naomi, call me Mara for the Almighty hath dealt very bitterly with me. I went out full, and the Lord hath brought me home again empty: why then call ye me Naomi, seeing the Lord hath testified against me, and the Almighty hath afflicted? So Naomi returned, and Ruth the Moabitess, her daughter in law, with her, which returned out of the country of Moab: and they came to Bethlehem in the beginning of barley harvest." When you are ready to get in a rage you need go to the Bible and read these scriptures. You need to shake yourself and tell yourself that you are not going to get like that. We need to start rebuking the devil and use the power that we have. What good is it to have power and not use it?  Don't let the devil rule your house.  You need to raise your window and say, "Devil you have been here long enough! Get out!" Don't allow him to take residence in your house. Cast him out of there and say, "No more anger, bitterness, malice, envy, jealousy, conceit and strife in this house!  You are getting out!"  Grab him by the seat of his pants and throw him out. Don't let the devil back in.  Don't let anger back in.  Evict it.  When you evict a person they are supposed to get out and stay out.  You are not supposed to let them back in and they are doing the same thing before you put them out.  Start laughing, smiling and praising the Lord around the house.  Start loving one another.  Get that spirit of anger out of there.  It can get in there so thick that you will be fighting to get it out.  Get that thing out of there.  Exterminate it.  Kill it!

When the people were saying, "Crucify Jesus!" they got mad.  They started throwing dust in the air.  People can stir up some stuff because they are bitter.  Jesus was not trying to bother anybody, but somebody put thoughts in their heads that He was dangerous. When they put lies in their heads about Jesus, they got their pick handles and wanted to hurt him. People can put things in your mind and say that people are no good. Those types of people are about nothing. Don't mess with them. The Bible says, "Woe unto them that wound their brother's weak conscience." They could have the utmost confidence in that person. But because of what you tell them they will think differently about that person.

Anything that is grevious is bitter. If it grieves you it is a bitter thing. Sometimes life tastes bitter when you drink it. Exodus 15:23-26 reads, "And when they came to Marah, they could not drink of the waters of Marah, for they were bitter: therefore the name of it was called Marah. And the people murmured against Moses saying, What shall we drink? And he cried unto the Lord; and the Lord shewed him a tree; which when he had cast into the waters, the waters were made sweet: there he made for them a statute and an ordinance, and there he proved them, and said, If thou wilt diligently hearken to the voice of the Lord thy God, and wilt do that which is right in his sight, and wilt give ear to his commandments, and keep all his statutes, I will put none of these diseases upon thee, which I have brought upon the Egyptians: for I am the lord that healeth thee." When life goes bad people start murmuring. You have to listen attentively to God and to His word. You have to keep all of his statutes. You have to keep everything in his word. He is not going to compromise for anybody. God told the people that they will live forever if they do what He tells them to. The only reason people get diseases and are sick is because they don't do what God tells them to do. God said he will heal them. His is Jehovah Rapha, the Lord that healeth thee. Some of us want God to work miracles in our lives. A blessing delayed is not a blessing denied. God delayed Daniels blessings for twenty one days, but it came.

People don't want to suffer. The Bible tells us to have patience to wait on the promise, after we have suffered a while. Job 10:1 says, "My soul is weary for my life; I will leave my complaint upon myself; I will speak in the bitterness of my soul." Job was bitter. He didn't blame it on anyone but himself. When you deal with your own bitterness you will come out with flying colors. You have to sweep around your own front door and keep your door clean. When our lives are clean we can see clearly to help someone else. Jesus called the people hypocrites because they had beams in their eyes and they were trying to be in someone else's eyes. You think that it is your brother's eye because it is so big, but it is really in your eye.

You can get in a fit of anger and say things that you are not supposed to say. I have gotten so mad at someone that I said that I wished that they would walk in front of a truck. I had to repent for that. Yes you do have to repent for saying things like that. Some people are so sanctified that they think they have already arrived. Saints talk like that when they are in a fit of anger. Nobody knows you are like that because you cover it up. Don't hold anything in your heart against your neighbor. We need to love our neighbors just like we love ourselves. The scripture doesn't say if they haven't done anything wrong or if they buy you gifts or give you things, then you are supposed to love them. It only simply tells us to love our neighbors. You have to love them even when they hate you and can't stand the ground you walk on. You have to love them.

# A Contentious Woman

A woman can be drop dead gorgeous, but when she opens her mouth and begins to talk and curse she is not beautiful anymore. Her mouth is nasty and dirty. She starts to look ugly. She curses like a sailor. You don't pay too much attention to a man when he curses, but when a woman curses, it messes up her whole demeanor. She is supposed to be dainty, sweet and cuddly. She is supposed to be lovable. She is not supposed to be brazen, boasting and ready to fight. She should be tender and not picking up baseball bats and knives to hurt somebody. You can be like that without being saved. It should come naturally. Women are not supposed to be fussing, cursing and always on edge. I am not saying that is what a man is supposed to do but that type of behavior is not appealing on a woman. The Bible tells us that a contentious woman is like water dropping on a rock. In time it will wear out.

Proverbs 21:9 reads, "It is better to dwell in a corner of the house top, than with a brawling woman in a wide house." A brawling woman is a contentious or angry woman. It is good if you have to dwell on the roof or in the corner of the house, than with a contentious and angry woman. It is also better to go into the forest or wilderness than to be with a contentious or angry woman. She always has something to say and she is never satisfied with anything. There are a lot of angry people in the world. They are angry because of things that have happened in her life. Jezebel got in trouble because she was messing with Elijah. Her husband was crying because of some land that Na'both the Jezreelite didn't sell him. She went and confronted Elijah, put fear in his heart and he ran. She already killed other prophets, so Elijah ran. Sisters, don't be brawlers and fighters. Be like Sarah, whose daughters you are. Sarah had a meek and quiet spirit. She was not a clamorous woman. Jezebel was a loud woman. She told Elijah what she was going to do to him. Some people will burn your bed if you are not careful.

Holy women are meek and quiet. They are not brazen nor boastful. They do not try to tell their husbands what to do. Let your husband be the head of the house. He can't run it if you don't let him. Let him deal with the hard issues. My ministers deal with the small issues of the church but I deal with the hard ones. If someone in the church has a small issue they go to one of the assistant pastors. If it is a serious or hard issue, such as sin, they come to me. If you have a meek and quiet spirit you are the daughter of Sarah. If you are brazen when you talk to the pastor, you will become so brave that you tell the pastor where to go. My wife can't tell me what to do in or out of the church. You cannot boss the man of God of your house around. You must follow his plan. He is the prophet of your house. The woman was made for the man, and not the man for the woman. You have to get out of the Women's Liberation era.

Proverbs 5:1-4 says, "My son, attend unto my wisdom, and bow thine ear to my understanding;

that thou mayest regard discretion, and that my lips may keep knowledge. For the lips of a strange woman drop as an honeycomb, and her mouth is smoother than oil. But her end is bitter than wormwood and sharp as a two edged sword. Her feet go down to death; her steps take hold to hell." You should be able to speak knowledge to someone else. A woman with a smooth mouth can trick you. What is smoother than oil? In the end, you will die naturally or spiritually. The woman in the scripture is a resident of hell. That is where she lives. Some women act like dudes. You can't be brawlers with an attitude. You must be gentle. It doesn't mean you are weak because you are meek. A foolish woman is loud and clamorous. Learn how to talk soft like a woman should. When you are loud like that the scripture, Proverbs 9:13, calls you simple and tells us that you know nothing.

# Lying

Put off the lying man with all his deeds. Everything that causes you to lie, put it off. Put on the new man. Put on holiness. Put on kindness and humbleness. God wants us to forgive one another. Don't be like that. It is not godly. Stop lying. We have saints that lie in the church. The book of Ephesians was written to the church. We are members one to another. Why would you want to lie? What's on your mind?

Stop lying to each other. Tell the truth and shame the devil. You can't say, "I was playing." No, you just lied. Saying, "psyche" is a lie too. A lie is an act to deceive. You try to deceive and trick someone to make them believe something else. The Bible says that all liars shall have their part in the lake of fire. "Church" liars as well as "world" liars will have their part. You have to get that lying out of your spirit. People just walk around making up lies. They lie just for the fun of it. There are peacemaking liars who lie to make peace. I am telling you right now that is not right. A lie is a lie, plain and simple.

Truth is not ready to be spoken at all times. Just because it is the truth doesn't mean it is time to say it. Sometimes you need to pray about it and leave it alone. Some people are not ready for the truth. You can't say everything even though it might be the truth. In the book of Ecclesiastes 3:1, "To everything there is a season, and a time to every purpose under the heavens." We try to tell people things because we are made. It may be the truth but you were mad when you said it. You hit that point because you are trying to make impact because you are upset. Most of the time people are in a vulnerable position and they can't handle the truth right then. If you pray for your enemies they might be ready for you to tell them the truth.

When a person lies to you with a straight face, they are deceitful. They won't even bat an eye.

They don't feel anything behind or feel any guilt. When the people where lying on Jesus, he didn't say a word. They were paid to lie on Jesus. Is anyone paying you to lie? Let people lie on you. God is your defense. There are people lying on me. I can feel their mouths moving. They hate this church because we are going somewhere. Watch people who say things and don't fulfill them. People say a whole lot of things and don't back up what they say. If you say you are going to do something then do it. If you are not going to do it then don't say it. God is not in the shady business that people are doing. If I tell you that I am going to do something then I will do it. When people say things that they are going to do and don't do it, they are not faithful. The Bible calls them wicked. Their words are wicked. Their throats are like graveyards. They have a very slick way of making you believe what they say. Watch those kinds of people. They are not real. There are people like that in the church. They have the works of the mind in their hearts. Some people lie all the time. They lie and think that they are telling the truth. God hates these things.

In Psalms 40:4 we read, "Blessed is that man that maketh the Lord his trust, and respecteth not the proud, nor such as turn aside to lies." Another scripture, Psalms 63:11 reads, "But the king shall rejoice in God; everyone that sweareth by him shall glory: but the mouth of them that speak lies shall be stopped." This scripture lets us know that God despises a lying tongue. When the scripture speaks about lying mouths being stopped, most of the time you're either dead or mute.

Psalms 101:7 reads, "He that worketh deceit shall not dwell within my house: he that telleth lies shall not tarry in my sight." This scripture tells us not to even think about stepping in His house if lies and deceit are part of our daily operations.

Don't lie to your brother. Tell the truth. It is easier to tell the truth than to lie. Don't be treacherous in your dealings. Don't go around packing lies around the church. Don't throw "rocks" and hide your hands. This type of activity

is in the church today. It might not seem like it is in your church, but it is. There is a type of rodent called a pack rat. He stores food in his mouth for months and then eats it. There are people who do the same thing with lies. When they want to tell them, they distribute them. The only thing that should be in your mouth is prayer. You are supposed to be saved. Saved people tell the truth and don't do these things. The devil will sometimes try to corner you and make you lie. You have to make the decision to tell the truth whether it hurts or not. Somebody tried to get me to talk about someone but I told them to get the information from the source. He tried to get me to lie on him and tried to put me on
me on the spot. My eyes are opened and my ears are tuned to discern what is right and wrong. The devil is my number one enemy. I don't need any more.

This scripture in Revelation sums it all up. Revelation 21:8 reads, "But the fearful, and unbelieving, and the abominable, and murderers, and whoremongers, and sorcerers, and idolater, and all liars, shall have their art in the lake which burneth with fire and brimstone: which is the second death." If you don't get it together with that scripture you need to ask God to give you a better understanding of His word and for the Holy Ghost.

# The Money Issue

The church needs money.  We are clothing the naked, going to the hospital to pray for the sick and going to the prisons to minister to the incarcerated.

The clerk at the gas and electric or water companies don't get questioned when they ask for their money for the previous month of service. When the landlord comes for the rent money or when the car company asks you for your car payment, you give it to them.  The reason why you are not questioning it is because it is something for you.  Would you question your boss if you worked all week and came to get your paycheck and he asked you, "Why are you coming in here asking for money?"  You will tell him that you worked for it and you will not let him keep your money.  If your overtime is messed up you, with the Holy Ghost, will say, "You messed up my overtime and I want my money!"

When the church asks for money people won't give it to them. The church is just trying to get people right with God. Isn't it strange how we pay so much money to be entertained and see sport figures, but can't support the house of God? Early in the morning they line up out the door for a good seat to see a baseball or football game. I like sports too but we take all of our money and support the various industries that are available to us. When it comes to the church we want to complain about it and ask questions like, "Why does the church keep asking for money?" You don't ask that question when you want to buy something. The store owner doesn't get questioned about his high prices. People say they don't like to go to church because every time they go the church asks for money. Every time you get your paycheck the government takes your money and you don't ask questions, so why ask questions when the church asks for money? The church is winning souls and feeding the hungry amongst other things.

Another thing that makes us bitter is debt. You can't do what you want because you don't have the money. We should tell ourselves to stay out of financial reverses. We should not be satisfied with the status quo. We should not always want to be broke.

There was a man who wanted his tithes back from the church. He even had the pastor in the news paper. People will try to embarrass you with the world. Another man did the same thing and got a leaping sickness and leaped right out into judgment. He tried to give his tithes back to the church but it was too late.

Some people don't pay tithes. Just because one spouse works doesn't mean that the other doesn't have to pay tithes if there are other sources of income in the household. The Bible tells us to pay tithes off of every increase. Malachi 3:10 reads, "Bring ye all the tithes in the storehouse that there may be meat in mine house, and prove me now herewith, saith the Lord of hosts, if I will not open you the windows of heaven and pour you out a blessing, that *there shall not be room enough to receive it.*"

Someone once told me that it was hard to pay tithes because they wouldn't have any other money coming in. If you stop buying everything, you will have it. There were times when I was broke, but I still had to pay my tithes. The Bible says that a tenth is holy unto the Lord. Does God need your tithes? No. God does not spend money. He needs it for ministry. If the people fund the ministry we can get souls and feed and clothe them. We can't do that if there is not an adequate amount of money coming in the church. You should never mess with your tithes. The Bible also tells us when we come into the house of God to bring an offering. In the book of Leviticus it tells us what to bring for offering right down to the baby. You have to give what God tells you to give.

Don't be around people who have any money. A preacher once said, "Isn't it strange how people spend money on what they want, but then they

want to beg the church for their rent. People
expect the church to pick up their tab. It is not
always possible to do that. It sometimes messes
up the church records. People will get angry
when you don't loan them any money. When I
used to ask my boss for small loans when I was
working he used to tell me that he wasn't a bank
institution. The same goes for the church.

People need to learn self control. If you learn
how to control your spending and not live above
your means, you can make it. Don't strike hands
with creditors. If you know you can't pay for it
right away, put it in layaway. There is nothing
wrong with putting things in layaway. However,
it is a bad thing to furnish your whole house on
credit and you can't pay for it. You know you
don't have enough credit but you get mad at the
loan officer when he doesn't loan you any money.
If you use your credit card, you have to pay for it.
It is best to cut your cards up. If you don't want
to do that then you must learn how to use them
responsibly.

Some people can't have a lot of money because they won't know how to manage it. You have to work extra hard to get more money. We often spend more money than we make. Some people can be filthy rich and not look like it. You will never know that he owns his own company. You will never know what they have. When some people get rich they want limousines with butlers and maids in them. They even shop at the high priced stores. I once went to a store here in Cincinnati called Wendell's. I thought I was doing something. I pulled my checkbook out and looked for a pair of lambskin shoes. One pair of those shoes was fifteen hundred dollars! I can't imagine paying that much for a pair of shoes. You better believe I put my checkbook right back in my pocket. The world lives very expensively. Somebody wrote a fifty million dollar check for a house they didn't want to wait two years for. Some people just have that kind of money. People who don't have a lot of money shouldn't spend a lot of money. When the man comes to repossess the car we want to hide it. Some of the men in that business have been killed for pulling peoples' car out of their driveways. Years ago, I was one day late on my car payment and they came to my job and repossessed my car.  They will not tell you when they are coming.  You should not be ashamed when that happens.  These things happen to the best of us.  Don't feel bad about it.  I have had cars repossessed but now I am in my blessed season.  It took some years of my cars being repossessed and my wages being garnished, but I don't have to worry about that anymore.  It also took some getting on my knees to get where I am now.

No amount of money is worth your soul.  Money will send some people to hell.  They love money so much that they will do anything to get it.  They will even rob their families to get money.  It is bad when mothers have to put their purses in the chair with them when they sit down.  My pastor once said that people will flip your sick body over to get to your money.  The Bible tells us that the love of money is the root of all evil.  It didn't say we couldn't have it.

We used to have revivals for the souls of men. Now we are having "possession" revivals. I've even heard of financial revivals. Where did that come from? They want everybody to come and bring money. All they do for the whole week is bring money. The Lord is looking for us to win souls for Him. Don't get me wrong, having money is fine and we can't operate the church properly without it but our main focus shouldn't be on money but on souls also. We need a soul winning revival. So, I ask the question, "What's on your mind?"

# <u>Hypocrisy</u>

Matthew 25:75 says, "And Peter remembered the words of Jesus, which said unto him, Before the cock crow, thou shalt deny me thrice. And he went out, and wept bitterly." God knows what we are thinking. He knows the intents of our heart and He knows what we intend to do. Peter told Jesus that he would go all the way with him. He even cut his ear off. When he remembered what Jesus said to him, he wept bitterly. We say we will live and die for the Lord. We jus better make sure we are fortified and mean what we say. We even sing in our prayers, "Lord I will live for you!" "Oh, Jesus!" We start calling off all of his names. He only wants us to call on the name of Jesus. We think we will be heard for much speaking. It sounds good to us and everybody else. He wants us to call on him when he is near. If you don't mean it then don't say it. He will come and make sure you mean what you say. He will also remind you of your prayer. When tribulation comes we need to make sure we will do what we say in our prayers. When Pete was running off at the mouth, Jesus told him that he was not speaking the things of God. Jesus had to go to the cross. If he didn't, there would be no chance for humanity. And because of that selfless act you have to tell the devil to get behind you. You are going all the way come hell or high water. I am not giving up now. It is too late in the game. You can't turn back and quit now. Wicked people already have a place reserved for them.

Righteous people have a place reserved for them too. Job 21:25-31 reads, "And another dieth in the bitterness of his soul, and never eateth with pleasure. They shall lie down alike in the dust, and the worms shall cover them. Behold, I know your thoughts, and the devices which ye wrongfully imagined against me. For ye say, Where is the house of the prince? And where are the dwelling places of the wicked? Have ye not asked them that go by the way? And do ye not know their tokens, that the wicked is reserved to the day of destruction?  They shall be brought forth to the day of wrath.  Who shall declare his way to his face?  And who shall repay him what he hath done?

We have to obey people who are in authority. If you don't you are being rebellious.  You have issues to deal with.  We all have to be subject to law enforcement.  If you are speeding or running stop signs you will get a ticket.  If you break the law you are going to jail.  If you break welfare laws you are going to jail.  Somebody kept throwing a way their bills and wouldn't pay attention to the advice his friends were giving him.  The I.R.S. got to him and took everything he had.  If you don't obey the laws of the land you will pay the consequences.  The Bible tells us that the law is for the lawless.  People who commit crimes go to jail.  You have to stand before a judge and approach him with "yes sir" and "no sir."  You can't go in the courtroom and talk any way you want to.  One man went into a courtroom and started talking crazy to the judge and the judge gave him ten years straight.  You cannot

take things into your own hands. Titus 3:1-9
reads, "Put them in mind to be subject to
principalities and powers, to obey magistrates, to
be ready to every good work, to speak evil of no
man, to be no brawlers, but gentle, shewing all
meekness unto all men. For we ourselves also
were sometimes foolish, disobedient, deceived,
serving divers lusts and pleasures, living in malice
an envy, hateful and hating one another. But after
that the kindness and love of God our Saviour
toward man appeared, not by works of
righteousness which we have done, but according
to his mercy he saved us, by the washing of
regeneration, and renewing of the Holy Ghost;
which he shed on us abundantly through Jesus
Christ our Saviour; that being justified by his
grace, we should be made heirs according to the
hope of eternal life. This is a faithful saying, and
these things I will that thou affirm constantly, that
they which gave believed in God might be careful
to maintain good works. These things are good
and profitable unto men. But avoid foolish
question, and genealogies, and contentions, and
strivings about the law; for they are unprofitable

and vain." Sometimes you have to suffer yourself
to be defrauded. You know that person is wrong.
This book is to help you get the works of the flesh
out of you because you always have to defend
yourself against your brother. Don't always feel
that you have to retaliate or say something back.
You don't always have to defend yourself. The
words that you speak out of your mouth will
either condemn or justify you. The words out of
your mouth will snare you. I tell my church not to
tell me anything that they are going to do unless
they mean it. When Jesus stood before Pilate he
didn't say a word. People hate my church
because we are going somewhere. I can feel their
mouths moving. After you
know the word of God you still should not be a
foolish person. You cannot have jealousy in your
heart and still. The devil will put jealousy in your
heart while you are right in the church. You can
speak in tongues and dance, but it won't be the
dance of the Lord. The devil can imitate tongues
but can't live anything. He can look holy and
transform himself into an angel of light. You
must live holy and you cannot have malice and

envy in your heart. Jealousy or envy will not
enter in the kingdom of God. Jesus is soon to
come. For years we have been preaching and
teaching about it but it is time to realize that the
rapture is soon to take place.

III John 1:10-14 says, "Wherefore, if I come, I
will remember his deed which he doeth, prating
against us with malicious words: and not content
therewith, neither doth he himself receive the
brethren, and forbade them that would, and
casteth them out the church. Beloved, follow not
that which is evil, but that which is good. He that
doeth good is of God: But he that doeth evil hath
not seen God. Demetrius hath good report of all
men, and of the truth itself: yea, and we also bear
record; and ye know that our record is true. I had
many things to write but I will not with ink and
pen write unto thee. But I trust I shall shortly see
thee, and we shall speak face to face. Peace be to
thee. Our friends salute thee. Greet the friends by
name." People don't want you to be in the church
but you have to be determined that no devil is
going to run you out of it. You are predestined to

be there. Everyone is not going to receive you.
They will get mad at you because people
you because people will befriend you when you
come in the church. Some people feel threatened
when new saints come into the church. If you are
doing what you are supposed to do you will not
feel threatened. I have young preachers under me
but I am not threatened because they can move a
little better than I can.

I Peter 2:1-9 reads, "Wherefore laying aside
all malice, and all guile, and hypocrisies, and
envies, and all evil speaking, as newborn babes,
desire the sincere milk of the word, that ye may
grow thereby: if so ye be have tasted that the Lord
is gracious. To whom coming, as unto a living
stone, disallowed indeed of men, but chosen of
God, and precious, ye also as lively stones, are
built up a spiritual house, an holy priesthood, to
offer up spiritual sacrifices, acceptable to God by
Jesus Christ. Wherefore also it is contained in the
scripture, behold, I lay in Sion a chief cornerstone,
elect, precious: and he that believeth on him shall
not be. Unto you therefore which

believe he is precious: but unto them which be disobedient, the stones which the builders disallowed, the same is made the head of the corner. And a stone of stumbling, and a rock of offence, even to them which stumble at the word, being disobedient: whereunto also they were appointed. But ye are a chosen generation, a royal priesthood, an holy nation, a peculiar people; that ye should shew forth the praises of him who hath called out of darkness into his marvelous light."

There are a lot of different hypocrisies going around. Some people are envious of other people. They don't like what they wear, how they look or even what kind of car they drive. God loves us. These are not his attributes. They are the attributes of the devil. We need to be like babies, how they desire the milk they need for nourishment we need to desire the word of God. One preacher said that we have religious midgets. Some people just wont grow up. You cannot provoke one another to anger. You are supposed to be holy. We are supposed to be saints not aints. Jesus is the chief cornerstone. People who don't obey the word of God, fall and stumble. If you

are obedient you will do everything the man of
God and the word of God says. Some people will
not obey anyone. They disregard the word of
God. If Jesus himself came down to preach they
wouldn't pay him any attention. Some people are
called to be disobedient. They are in the church
just to aggrevate the pastor. Everybody is not in
church to be saved. They are there to be a thorn
in the pastor's side. Until the pastor gets the
victory over them, they will not leave. There was
one sister who used to come into the pulpit ragged
and disheveled. The pastor tried to talk to her but
she would never listen to him. He put her out of
the pulpit but every Sunday she would come back
to embarrass him. The Lord told him that until he
got the victory over her and stopped worrying
about her, she will not leave. When he stopped
worrying, she left and never came back. You
never know what your test is going to be. Go
through the test to make you a better person. We
are a royal priesthood. We are children of the
King. You should show forth his praises. You
should praise God when you are in and out of the
church.

I Peter 2:16-25, "As free, and using your liberty
for a cloke of maliciousness, but as the servants of
God. Honour all men. Love the brotherhood.
Fear God. Honour the king. Servants, be subject
to your masters with all fear, not only to the good
and gentle, but also to the forward. For this is
thankworthy, if a man for conscience toward God
endure grief, suffering wrongfully. For what
glory is it, if, when ye be buffeted for your faults,
ye shall take it patiently? But if, when ye do well,
and suffer for it, ye take it patiently, this is
acceptable with God. For even hereunto were ye
called: because Christ also suffered for us, leaving
an example, that ye should follow his steps. Who
did no sin, neither was guile found in his mouth.
Who, when he was reviled, reviled not again;
when he suffered, he threatened not; but
committed himself to him that judgeth
righteously. Who his own self bare our sins in his
own body on the tree that we, being dead to sins,
should live unto righteousness: by whose stripes
ye were healed. For ye were as sheep going
astray; but are now returned unto the Shepherd
and Bishops of your souls." Don't use your

liberty to do malicious things.  We need to endure
grief and bitterness for our mind's sake.  We
sometimes have to suffer wrong to stay right.
You have to take ridicule and being run down.
The flesh will sometimes rise up.  Now the Ghost
is taking care of your business.  Let the Holy
Ghost handle it.  This book is written to help you
face the outside world.  When we leave the church
environment we don't want to act like saints
anymore.  When we are beat up spiritually
sometimes we deserve it because we do things
that we shouldn't do.  All you have to do is take
life patiently.  God tells us to be patient when
people flip on us.  It is acceptable to him.  When
they talked about Jesus, it hurt him.  They talked
about his mother, Mary.  They called him a
bastard.  We say, "Sticks and stones will break my
bones but words will never hurt me."  That is not
true.  When there are things said about us they
hurt.  Jesus is our perfect example because he did
not lash back out at them.  When these things
come to face to us can we tell the person, "God
bless you?"  We should follow in the steps of
Jesus.  We need to live what we preach.  The devil
will try you as soon as you walk out the door.  He

will push the button that he knows he shouldn't push. He knows what will get you on edge.

If you are around people that are always fussing, get away from them. They will have you fussing. They will mess up your spirit. Evil communication corrupt good manner. You may be a good person that does not argue or fuss, but if you are in the company of them that do, you will start too. They don't even obey the truth. They don't want to hear the truth about themselves. It's alright if the finger is pointed at someone else, but if it is pointed at them they don't want to hear it. If you can't get the help you need through Bible class then you need to talk to someone who is unbiased and doesn't know you. You need serious help. If the word of God can't dig it out of you, you need help. God has no respect of persons. If there are things that you are trying to hide, God will open it up. You can't hide from God's eyes. He sees everything open, naked and bare. You might try to fool the man of God sometimes, but you can't fool God anytime. You will be judged by what comes out of your pastor's mouth.

The devil can do signs and wonders to make you believe he is God. People don't want to hear about the love of God and truth. They will fight you tooth and nail about it. The reason why God will do what he is going to do is because people don't love the truth. Do you love the truth? The truth is, we still have the works of the mind in us. We don't want to get rid of them. We still want to act like babies. It is time to come out of the baby stage. We need to take off the diapers and stop drinking milk and start eating meat. We want someone to pat our backs all the time.

II Thessalonians 2:11-12 says, "And for this cause God shall send them a strong delusion, that they should believe a lie. That they all might be damned who believed not the truth, but had pleasure in unrighteousness." There are people who would rather believe a lie than realize the truth to stay in their comfort zone. Once you release or let go of your sin you can't go back to it. You can sit right in the church and be delusional. I tell my people all the time, if anyone goes to hell in this church it won't be anybody's

fault but theirs.  If you are saved you shouldn't
have pleasure in unrighteous things.  You can
only imitate it for so long.  Then it wears off.  If
you are saved then you should live right all the
time.

Some people are swift to shed innocent blood.
They love misery.  They want you to be miserable
with them.  The old saying is, "Misery loves
company."  I like to be around happy people.  I
had enough misery when I was in sin.  It is up to
you to be happy and not miserable.  The ball is in
your court.  When the ball is thrown to you, it is
your turn to shoot it.  Let no one determine how
you are supposed to feel and how your joy should
flow.  I don't care how anyone act I still have my
joy.  I don't care who doesn't like me.  This joy
that I have, the world didn't give it and I have, the
world didn't give it and the world can't take it
away!  If you have the Holy Ghost, rivers of joy
should be flowing.  Stagnated waters should not
be coming out.  Your hope is in God and nobody
else.  David said, "I will yet praise him!"  We
have been through hell and high water and still
have our joy.  People don't know what you are

going through but you still have your joy. The devil is trying to mess with you but you still have your joy. Your mind can't be boggled down because you still have your joy. Your joy is stronger than anything the devil is trying to put on you. The devil may try to set you off course but you need to keep your joy. He can derail your life. When your life is derailed, people get hurt. It is a very serious thing for a train to be on course. The devil doesn't want you to be on course. Don't get side tracked. What's on your mind? You should be tired of doing the same things that get you off course. We need God to help us. The devil messes with your mind and you can't get things straight. Every time you get your mind straight the devil knocks you off course. Tell the devil you are not going to do the things that he wants you to. It is alright to say no sometimes. If you don't say no, people will take advantage of you.

The devil doesn't want you to get on the Holy Ghost train to heaven. There are two trains that are leaving here. The first train is the midnight train where the devil will cause trouble. When you go through the tunnel you transfer to the second train, which is the morning train. It will not be late. You have to have your ticket ready. Your ticket is the fruits of the spirit. The works of the mind ticket is null and void. You don't want to have that ticket. It is the ticket to hell. People do not have the fear of God in their hearts. They do not care. We all have sinned and come short of the glory of God. Whatever you used to do for the Lord and don't do now is a sin. Being disobedient is a sin. If you don't read your Bible like you used to, it is a sin. Unbelief is disobedience. You used to care about God but don't care for him anymore. We don't love God like we used to. We love other things. We have left him alone by himself. He is wondering where his bride is. She is gone off with another man. The other man is things.

There is a time when you should meditate on the word of God. Think on his blessings, his goodness and what he is getting ready to do in your life. If you are not where God wants you right now, think on how you will get to where he wants you to be. We have a class going on at our church called "God Chasers" based on the book by Tommy Tenney. We all need to chase God. We are so far from him it is not funny. If we weren't so far away we wouldn't have to chase him and act like we do. People who are close to God don't act crazy. There are secret places in God for us to abide in where the devil can't mess with our minds. The Bible tells us that if we dwell in the secret places of the most High God, we will abide under the shadow of the Almighty.

If you have the works of the mind in you, God will show you up. If you are close to God you are obedient. You will find that disobedient people will do anything. God gets happy when your spirit is quiet and you meditate on him. People will get on your last nerve but you will not let the works of the mind show. You will cut the root down before they grow. If you don't cut your weeds down they will grow so high, they will choke your flowers. They reason why the weeds grow so high is because you don't take care of them. The works of the mind creep up in our lives because we don't pull them up with the word of God. Dandelions will kill your grass. They may look pretty but they are bad for your lawn. The devil will make you think you told somebody off and showed them up. Those things feel good to the flesh to get in a rage and defend yourself. We act like it doesn't feel good. You don't care who you hurt when you say bad things to people. There is a garden tool called The Claw that digs roots up. That is how the word of God is. You are going to have some holes in your life for a while until the Holy Ghost starts filling them back up. The Holy Ghost will go down there and take those roots up and fill your holes with some joy.

We have to run from evil. Get away from things that don't look or feel right. The eyes of the Lord are over the righteous. God hears you when you do righteous things. He does not hear you when you are doing wicked things. God will hear your prayers when you are doing right. You can take a camera and follow me around and you will see that my life is not different. When he saved me, he saved me completely. You will not find me creeping in and out of bars and clubs. You won't catch me riding around somewhere that I have no business being. You can get in trouble that way. God's judgment is against those that do evil. I don't want God against me. We are fighting the devil and his demons. We shouldn't want God against us. I can't imagine God being my enemy. You might as well dig yourself a hole and jump in it. No one can harm you if you do good. Get happy when you suffer for righteousness sake. Set God inside your heart and mind. What's on your mind? Is it God or to do something wrong. You don't have to do anything wrong. You can live holy. It is the Holy Ghost that causes men and women to live right. You can't live right without it. In the book of Peter it tells us we have hope in God. We need to be meek and have reverence for God. People with the works of the mind do not have a good conscience. They can't sleep at night. They toss and turn because the devil is taunting them. The works of the mind are demons. People don't like to live holy. If you do, they will falsely accuse you.

I Peter 3:8-22 reads, "Finally, be ye all of one mind, having compassion one of another, love as brethren, be pitiful, be courteous. Not rendering evil for evil, or railing for railing: but contrariwise blessing; knowing that ye are thereunto called, that ye should inherit a blessing. For he that will love life, and see good days, let him refrain his tongue from evil and his lips that they speak no guile. Let him eschew evil, and do good; let him seek peace, and ensue it. For the eyes of the Lord are over the righteous, and his ears are open unto their prayers: but the face of the Lord is against them that do evil. And who is he that will harm you, if ye be followers of that which is good? But and if ye suffer for righteousness' sake, happy are ye: and be not afraid of their terror, neither be troubled. But sanctify the Lord God in your hearts: and be ready always to give an answer to every man that asketh you a reason of the hope that is in you with meekness and fear: having a good conscience; that, whereas they speak evil of you, as of evildoers, they may be ashamed that falsely accuse your good conversation in Christ. For it is better, if the will of God be so, that ye suffer for well doing, than for evil doing. For Christ also hath once suffered for sins, the just for the unjust, that he might bring us to God, being put to death in the flesh, but quickened by the

Spirit: by which also he went and preached unto the spirits in prison; which sometime were disobedient, when once the longsuffering of God waited in the days of Noah, while the ark was a preparing, wherein few, that is, eight souls were saved by water. The like figure whereunto even baptism doth also now save us (not the putting away of the filth of the flesh, but the answer of a good conscience toward God,) by the resurrection of Jesus Christ: who is gone into heaven, and is on the right hand of God; angels and authorities and powers being made subject unto him."

The Bible says that a fool doesn't want to hear this kind of teaching. Proverbs 1:20-28 reads, "Wisdom crieth without; she uttereth her voice in the streets. She crieth in the chief place of concourse, in the openings of the gates: in the city she uttereth her words, saying, "How long, ye simple ones, will ye love simplicity? And the scorners delight in their scorning, and fools hate knowledge? Turn you at my reproof: behold I will pour out my spirit unto you, I will make known my words unto you. Because I have called, and ye refused; I have stretched out my hand, and no man regarded; but ye have set at nought all my counsel, and would none of my reproof: I also will laugh at your calamity; I will mock you when fear cometh as a whirlwind; when distress and anguish cometh upon you. Then they shall call upon me, but I will not answer; they shall seek me early, but they shall not find me."

People don't want to reveal what is on their minds because once they get the knowledge that they can't co it anymore they don't want to give it up. Don't get mad when the man of God reproves you. If you do you need to check if the Holy Ghost or your flesh is ruling. When the man of God reproves you then turn from whatever you were doing. Fix the situation. Get on your knees and get it right with God. God is stretching out his hand and nobody is reaching for it. You have a monkey on your back if you disobey the man of God. God will not hear your prayers if you disobey the man of God. I don't want God to turn his ear from me. I need him to hear me when I pray.

# Compassion and Forgiveness

Ephesians 4:32 reads, "And be ye kind one to another, tenderhearted, forgiving one another, even as God for Christ's sake hath forgiven you." Learn to cry for one another. We are in heavenly places because God has forgiven us. Learn how to be kind to somebody. People don't have to always come to you, you should go to them. You can build yourself a reputation of being mean and nasty. I wouldn't want anyone saying that about me. Then you get an attitude saying, "I don't care what they say." You should care what they say. Everyone leaves when you come around because you are mean. Everybody needs friends. Not to manipulate, but to be friends. We are talking about what comes out of the heart.

We need to learn how to do kind things for someone else other than ourselves. We have to learn how to forgive one another. If we don't then we won't make it to heaven. Get mad at yourself and say, "I am not going to be angry, but I am going to forgive." Forgive and forget. Go on so you can grow. You cannot grow if you are harvesting things in your heart. Forgive the people who have wounded you years ago and move on. Give them a call. If you can't forgive them, you have not dealt with your anger. You still have bitterness in you. You are still full of malice. You still hate them. You still have wrath in you, and you are still dealing with envy and jealousy. You are also conceited and stuck on your-self.

God wants us to forgive one another. If we are not forgiving then we are not godly. Christ forgave us, why can't we forgive? Make charity your daily clothes. Put it on. Put on love. When you put on love, you are right there on perfectness. When you are forgiving, loving, kind, humble, merciful and longsuffering you have the peace of God. Let the peace of God rule in your house. Let the word of Christ dwell in you richly. If it is in you richly, you won't be tripping. Sing with grace in your hearts to the Lord. We don't always know how to be kind. It is not hard to be kind. You should always be kind. We need to learn how to be tenderhearted to someone else. Show someone else sympathy. We have to forgive one another whether we want to or not. You can't go to heaven unless you forgive your brother. Your "brother" can be your wife, husband, sister, natural brother, etc. It is any person that you come in contact with.

Colossians 3:12 says, "Put on therefore, as the elect of God, holy and beloved, bowels of mercies, kindness, humbleness of min, meekness and longsuffering. You must be merciful. You have to have a very humble mind. You can't be arrogant and saved. You cannot be a saint of God and be like that. You must work on yourself and allow yourself to be meek, longsuffering and not be impatient with people. You have to have all those qualities to even be a pastor. Even though you know they are wrong, you still have to be patient. Jesus chose twelve disciples and told them that one of them was the devil. You may wonder why Jesus had Judas as the treasurer knowing that he was stealing money. Matthew was the accountant and tax collector. He let Judas

be the treasurer, until he hung himself. God will
give you space to repent, but if you don't you will
go head long into judgment. Bishop Cohen would
often say, "You might get by, but you won't get
away." Solomon said, "Sow your wild oats young
man/woman, but know this, judgment is coming."
If we don't get rid of all these things, it will stop
us from making the rapture. One of the most
critical issues in the church is that we don't know
how to forgive one another. It is a comfort zone
for us to hold unforgiveness in our hearts. We
feel good when we don't forgive. Unforgiveness
is a sin. If you don't forgive your brother, you are
in sin. If you are in sin, you can't go to heaven.
Jesus tell us before we bring our gifts to the altar,
we are to forgive. If you don't forgive, the devil
will get in there and blow it up. It will become a
big fire. If you had a big argument, then you need
to forgive. Don't always be the last one to say
I'm sorry. Get your sorry off first. If you say
sorry and keep up the fuss, you are not really
sorry. Some people say I'm sorry and don't mean
it. When a person says sorry and repents, they
stop arguing. They don't go back to doing it
again. Start learning how to love and not hate.

Hate is the devils spirit. When you love you have peace. If you are always angry, check your love life out. The Holy Ghost is love. When you are saturated with the Holy Ghost you will have no problem loving someone. You have to first love yourself, and when that is accomplished you can love somebody else. A lot of people don't love themselves. You have to look in the mirror and say, "I love me." Love comes from within the mind. If the word of God is in us richly, we can love one another. Love doesn't fight or argue with itself. If you put love deep in your heart you will be sweet. That is how it is supposed to be in the church.

Matthew 5:23 tells us to get it right with our brothers and sisters, and then offer our gifts to the Lord. We need to get our lives right and our minds clear. We must wash ourselves by the water and the word of God.

Matthew 5:11 says, "Blessed are ye, when men shall revile you, persecute you and say all manner of evil against you falsely, for my sake, rejoice and be exceedingly glad." They know they are hurting you but you still have to pray for them. Don't pray on your enemy, pray for them. I had to pray for someone that hurt me by what they said. I could not shake it, but I did with the help of my wife. People will have you angry and wanting to call them back, but I didn't. I had some kin people call me and tell me that I should be ashamed because I didn't let someone stay with me. At the time I had eight children in the home and no space to spare. He wanted to stay in my basement, but I didn't know what his intentions were. I love you but you can't stay here. People will try to make you feel bad because they are wrong. How can you impose on someone with eight kids, when you are a single man? I once took in my sister-in-law with her seven children so that made fifteen children in the house. I didn't want to see them on the streets. I took them in, but I won't take in a single man with no children. I don't play favorites with family members and because of that they get mad at me. What's on your mind? They are mad at me right now. If you are wrong then deal with it.

Some of us are hooked on kin people. They call my house trying to "straighten" me out. You find yourself on dangerous ground when you do that. Just because I am your blood, that doesn't mean anything. You don't know what danger you are in when you try to blast the man of God out. When you don't recognize what position others hold in the church, you will be disrespectful. You can't say anything you want to say. I pray that God will have mercy on them.

The word of God tells us in Romans 13:8-14, "Owe no man anything, but love one another: for he that loveth another hath fulfilled the law. For this, thou shalt not commit adultery, thou shalt not steal, thou shalt not bear false witness, thou shalt not covet; and if there be any other commandment, it is briefly comprehended in this saying namely, thou shalt love thy neighbour as thyself. Love worketh no ill to his neighbour: therefore love is the fulfilling of the law. And that, knowing the time, that now is high time to wake out of sleep: for now is our salvation nearer than we believed. The night is far spent, the day is at hand: let us therefore cast off the works of darkness and let us put on the armour of light. Let us walk honestly, as in the day; not in rioting and drunkenness, not in chambering and wantonness, not strife and envying. But put ye on the Lord Jesus Christ, and make not provision for the flesh, to fulfill the lust thereof."

Romans 12:10-21 says, "Be kindly affectionate one to another with brotherly love; in honour preferring one another. Not slothful in business; fervent in spirit; serving the Lord; rejoicing in hope;
patient in tribulation; continuing instant in prayer; distributing to the necessity of saints; given to hospitality. Bless them that persecute you; bless and curse not. Rejoice with them that do rejoice, and weep with them that weep. Be of the same mind one toward another. Mind not high things, but condescend to men of low estate. Be not wise in your own conceits. Recompense to no man evil for evil. Provide things honest in the sight of all men. Dearly beloved, avenge not yourselves, but rather give place unto wrath: for it is written,

vengeance is mine I will repay, saith the Lord. Therefore if thine enemy hunger, feed him; if he thirst, give him drink: for in so doing thou shalt heap coals of fire on his head. Be not overcome of evil, but overcome evil with good." You are supposed to bless people, not blast them. Don't be a person that is full of revenge. People who are full of revenge are full of bitterness. They are hateful. Don't render evil for evil. Don't pray that God will get them. God will get you for praying a prayer like that. He tells us to pray for our enemies. You know that people are using you. You see them using you, but God tells us to pray for them that despitefully use you and say all manner of evil against you for His names sake. But it has to be a false accusation. Something happened to me a few weeks ago, but my wife told me not to stoop to their level. My flesh wanted to and the devil tried to get me to, right before Bible Class. Sometimes you need someone to tell you not to do certain things.

Get happy with people when they are happy. Don't get mad when they are happy. Let the spirit of happiness and joy consume you. When they weep, let them know that you understand and weep with them.

There was a man who took his puppy and said, "I love you", in a mean tone. He opened his hand and the puppy ran like crazy. When the puppy came back he said, "I hate you", so nice and the puppy ran back into his hands. The point that I am trying to make is that, it is not what you say, but how you say it. If I ask you to pick up a piece of paper in the right way, you'll be glad to do it for me. It is the tone that you use. Let love be without dissimulation. Shout with them that shout. Rejoice with them that rejoice. Cry with them when they cry. What's on your mind? Don't be wise in your own slickness. Don't pay nobody back for the wrong they have done to you. Make sure everything you do is honest. Try to avoid conflict and live in peace. You don't have to show your ugliness all the time. Be nice. Don't be crazy with people. That same person might have to help you one day. There are people who hate me because I am the pastor. I might have to pray for them one day. I can't be a striker nor can I avenge myself. I have a God who is fighting for me. With the help of the Lord we will get the works of the flesh out of us.

Romans 13:7-9 says, "Render therefore to all their dues: tribute to whom tribute is due: custom to whom custom; fear to whom fear; honour to whom honour. Owe no man anything, but to love one another: for he that loveth another hath fulfilled the law. For this, thou shalt not commit adultery, thou shalt not steal, thou shalt bear false witness, thou shalt not covet; and if there be any other commandment, it is briefly comprehended in this saying, namely, thou shalt love thy neighbor as thyself." Don't owe any man anything but love. You will always be in debt to your neighbor for love. It is a good thing to owe your neighbor love. Do you love yourself? If you do you should love your neighbor. You can't love yourself and hate your neighbor. Your neighbor can be your husband, wife or anybody. Some people hate their children. Is that on your mind? Love doesn't do anything crazy to its neighbor.

Knowing that the time is short, we should be heaping love on one another. Stop sleeping and start loving.

You have to love and have mercy on people. People have more pity on animals than human life. I love animals. I have always been an animal lover. Society will kill a full term baby, but save the whales. There is no regard for human life at all. People will take human life and spill its blood, but will not harm a cat. I am not saying that you should harm a cat because if you do you are breaking the law but killing babies should also be against the law. The city of Nineveh had people who didn't know right from wrong but Jonah wanted God to destroy them. What kind of spirit do you have if you want God to kill somebody? Something is wrong with you. You shouldn't pray that God will kill or cripple your boss to get a raise. You will be surprised by what is on people's mind. If you don't let the Holy Ghost control your mind, you will be thinking all kinds of crazy thoughts. God was concerned about the cattle in Nineveh. If he killed them

Nineveh would have nothing to eat. We have to have compassion on everybody and everything. People act crazy sometimes but we still have to love them. You can't go to heaven if you don't love them. You are required by God to love them. They might not stand your guts but you have to love them.

The Holy Ghost is love. If you want to see someone dead or you don't love everybody, you are not going to heaven. You are literally wasting your time. You might as well get some liquor and marijuana and go back into the world. God tells us to love our neighbor as ourselves. You cannot be a minister, preacher or deacon, or whatever position you hold in the church, and not love everybody. You can love them when you know that they don't like you. I can still love the preachers that hate my guts. They don't like me because I refuse to take down and because of the way that I preach.

We should be helping those who need help. We get our children new things, which is not a problem, but the mother without a father in the house with a lot of children needs our help also. We need missionaries to go into homes, help comb the children's hair and help clean or straighten up their homes with their permission. You might say that they are nasty but they are in sin and sometimes they don't know any better. Can we help them with their children if they want us to? Can we go into their houses and help them clean up? Can we go and give them a home bible study? These are the things that we need to do. We need to feed people before we preach to them. When God fed the people before he preached to them, his disciples tried to push them away but he told them not to because he wanted to preach to them.

They ate naturally so they needed to eat spiritually.

Jeremiah 6:26 says," O daughter of my people, gird thee with sackcloth, and wallow thyself in ashes: make thee mourning, as for an only son, most bitter lamentation: for the spoiler shall suddenly come upon us." Peter wept bitterly because he denied Christ. He was sorry for what he did. We need to weep bitterly for the souls of men. We need to ask the Lord to help and save them. Isaiah 33:5-8 reads, "The Lord is exalted; for he dwelleth on high: he hath filled Zion with judgment and righteousness. And wisdom and knowledge shall the stability of the times, and strength of salvation: the fear of the Lord is his treasure. Behold their valiant ones shall cry without: the ambassadors of peace shall weep bitterly. The highways lie waste, the wayfaring man ceaseth: he had broken the covenant, he hath despised the cities, he regarded no man." We should weep bitterly because the highway of holiness is torn up. We should weep bitterly for the apostolic highways because men are tearing it up. They are destroying them. The wayfaring man or the fool is destroying our highways because they don't know which way to go. Souls don't know where to go, because men have moved the old ancient landmark. What's on your mind? Because of this, men and women of God should weep bitterly for the souls of men.

You should have mercy on somebody sometimes. Have mercy for someone else's family. Jesus wept at the tomb of Lazarus. The Bible says, "Blessed are the merciful for they shall obtain mercy." You can't walk around here coldhearted, with no mercy for anyone. Where is your Holy Ghost? Jesus was moved with compassion many times throughout the Bible. Why can't we be moved on a daily basis? Only when we are in trouble is when we want someone to have mercy on us. If you don't have mercy on anybody God will not have mercy on you.

We need to love as brethren. Have pity on someone other than yourself. If someone else is dealing with some things, have pity on them. Don't be nosey. Just tell them that you will fast for them so God can move in their life and make things better. We need to have compassion on each other. Don't just say the word, act on it. When God sees you having compassion on someone else He will bless you. We need to cover each other. The only way to cover one another is through fasting and prayer. We need to

lay before God and ask him to help us. We need
to pray to God and ask him to help us get these
devils off our back and get financial demons out
of our lives. Will you please pray for someone?
We need God to put compassion in our hearts.
Where we are lacking and don't have it He needs
to put it there. Don't only have compassion on
your friends but have compassion on someone
that you can't get along with. When you do that
God will start rooting things out of your life and
start fixing things up. In order to get to that point,
you have to be a God chaser. You can't chase
him today and not tomorrow. You have to
apprehend God to see what he has on his mind for
you.

One thing about my sons that I can say is that
they love one another. Because they love each
other they can love other people who are not their
blood. We can't look down on one another. We
are all in the same boat together. If we don't help
one another, we will sink together. When Peter
tells us to refrain from evil things, he was talking
to the church and not the sinners. Kind words

turn away wrath, but grievous words stir up strife. Say something kind to someone so you can turn away the anger, stress and wrath.

God gives us these scriptures and lets us hear and read the word of God because he loves us and wants us to be saved. The Bible tells us that God knows that we are his disciples if we love one another. That is the only way the sinner man is going to know us. We have to love people no matter what. It doesn't matter what you do. Love is stronger than hate. Don't love at church and not love at home or on your job. The Bible reminds us that while we were yet sinners, Christ loved and died for us. The question that I have for you is, "What's on your mind?"

# <u>Marriage</u>

Colossians 3:18 says, "Wives submit yourselves unto your own husbands, as it is fit in the Lord. Husbands, love your wives and be not bitter against them." The Bible tells the wives to submit, or be obedient, to your own husband. As a husband you must love your wife and not be bitter against her. You have to keep joy and love her anyhow. The Bible has something for all of us, even the children. He tells them to obey their parents. He tells the wives to submit first because he knows how they are. Some women can nag, nag, nag. You don't want to be a nag. He tells the husbands not to be bitter from her nagging. She nags you but don't hate and be bitter against her. Nagging can make your husband bitter.

The Bible also tells the wives in I Peter 3:1-7, "Likewise ye wives, be in subjection to your own husbands; that, if any obey not the word, they also may without the word be won by the conservation of the wives; while they behold your chaste conversation coupled with fear. Whose adorning let it not be that outward adorning of plaiting the hair, and wearing of gold, or of putting on apparel; But let it be the hidden man of the heart, in that which is not corruptible, even the ornament of a meek and quiet spirit, which is the sight of God of great price. For after this manner in the old time the holy women also, trusted in God, adorned themselves, being in subjection unto their own husbands: even as Sara obeyed Abraham, calling him lord: whose daughters ye are, as long as ye do well, and are not afraid with any amazement. Likewise, ye husbands, dwell with them according to knowledge, giving honour unto the wife, as unto the weaker vessel, and as being heirs together of the grace of life; that your prayers be not hindered. Finally, be ye of one mind, having compassion one of another, love as brethren, be pitiful, be courteous: Not rendering evil for evil, or railing for railing: but contrariwise blessing; knowing that ye are thereunto called, that ye should inherit a blessing.

An argumentative wife is like water dropping on a rock. It will wear it out. Don't be a contentious wife. The reason people don't like to get rid of the works of the mind is because, they won't have anything to argue about. If they confess it, they won't have to worry about it and the devil can't bother them anymore. Confess and forsake it. If you do, the Bible tells us that you shall have mercy. Something that you gather during the day on your job, you take it out on your husband or wife when you get home. You just nag, nag, nag and it get old. It will make your spouse fall out of love with you real quick. He will put on his hat and leave. Someone else will make him feel like a man. If you don't rub his head and massage his shoulders, someone else will. If you don't cook for him, someone else will cook for him just what he wants. Men need just as much of everything that women do. You are the one who sets the atmosphere in your home. If you have a house full of "frogs", then it stinks. Nobody wants to come home to a house full of frogs. That is not good.

God wants one man for one woman, forever. We weren't taught that growing up. We were taught that more than one relationship is alright. Every time you have a relationship with someone you give them a part of you. Before it's all over there is hardly anything left of you. Until you are completely delivered from your past relationships that didn't mean you any good, you cannot have a successful marriage.

The head of every man is Christ and not the woman. The head of the man is Christ. Wives need to stop wearing the husband's pants and men need to stop wearing their wives skirts. Stand up and be a man and do what you need to do. Wives, follow your man. The man of God's job would be a lot easier. I Corinthians 11:1-19 reads, "Be ye followers of me, even as I am of Christ. Now I praise you, brethren, that ye remember me in all things, and keep the ordinances, as I delivered them to you. But I would have you know that the head of every man is Christ; and the head of the woman is the man; and the head of Christ is God. Every man praying or prophesying, having his head covered, dishounoreth his head. But every woman that prayeth or prophesieth with her head uncovered, dishounoreth her head: for that is even all one as if she were shaven. For if the woman be not covered, let her also be shorn: but if it be a shame for a woman to be shorn or shaven, let her be covered. For a man indeed ought not to cover his head, forasmuch as he is the image and glory of God: but the woman is the glory of the man. For the man is not of the woman; but the woman of the man. Neither was the man created for the woman;

but the woman for the man. For this cause ought the woman to have power on her head because of the angels. Nevertheless neither is the man without the woman, neither the woman without the man, in the Lord. For as the woman is of the man, even so is the man also by the woman; but all things of God. Judge in yourselves: is it comely that a woman pray unto God uncovered? Doth not even nature itself teach you, that, if a man have long hair, it is a shame unto him? But id a woman have long hair, it is a glory to her: for her hair is given her for a covering. But if any man seem to be contentious, we have no such custom, neither the churches of God. Now in this that I declare unto you I praise you not, that ye come together not for the better, but for the worse. For first of all, when ye come together in the church, I hear that there be divisions among you: and I partly believe it. For there must be also heresies among you that they which are approved may be made manifest among you."

Wives, you make your husband look good. You are supposed to compliment him. You are the glory of your husband. My wife makes me look real good. If you look frayed and ugly and don't care how you present yourself then you make your husband look just as bad as you do. If you are glowing and doing right, you will make him stick out his chest. Be his glory and not his shame. Angels are in your house looking at you. The devil is also looking. He is seeing if you are going to do the right thing. Don't get the works of the mind out one day, and then put them back in the next day. You have to forebear one another. One side can't cooperate with the other if they don't want to. Life is what you make it. You are supposed to make your home comfortable for your husband when he is tired. I like to come home after a long, hard day at work. When I do I can just fall on the bed with clean sheets on them. I don't like going to bed on dirty sheets. It is the wife's job to take care of those things. Some women don't want to do that. Women are not slaves, but it is their duty. It's that that he doesn't have any hands, but run his bathwater sometimes. It used to be that the man would bring home the bread and the butter. It has gotten so heavy that now the woman has to work too because we have accumulated so many bills. The woman's place is supposed to be at home. Because of the Women's Liberation Era and the burning of bras, the home is not their place anymore. There are women slinging garbage and sledgehammers. It really does something to me to see that. Women are supposed to be soft, gentle and smooth to the touch. I am not talking about the barefoot and pregnant mentality. I'm talking about the husbands respecting your wives in the home. They are not your slaves. Every once in a while you can cook a meal for him. Make him want to come home. It is a shame if he has to sit in the car and wonder if he wants to come in the house or not. If your husband gives you a card, accept it. It doesn't have to have any money in it. Sometimes he might need a card just to say I love you. It might not happen all the time but sometimes is nice. It's a partnership thing. There are women and playboys out there that will lure your husband/wife. You better love him/her. Learn how to forgive one another.

My wife and I help each other out. The Bible says that we are workers together with Him. I might be the pastor but I still vacuum the floor and take out the trash. My wife and I go to the laundromat together. It does not make you less than a man to be seen in the laundromat with your wife. It is a good thing to spend time with her and talk to each other. You can't try to flatter anyone else's spouse. Flatter your own. Don't talk and smile at anyone else's spouse and not talk and smile at your own. That's

**What's On Your Mind?** 128

not right. It is a mutual thing. You have to treat
each other right.

Wives be under subjection to your own
husband. You will listen to someone else's
husband and won't listen to your own. There is
something wrong somewhere. In chapter thirteen
we read how people have no fear of God. They
walk in the house of the Lord mad and fussing
with their face all torn up. They think it is a
game. It is not a game. A lot of people will not
purchase this book because they do not want
anyone to tell them what is on their mind. They
don't want to hear the truth about themselves.
Preachers do not want to hear about themselves.
People do not want to hear the truth but want to
worry the man of God about things and put gray
hairs in his head before it is time for them to grow
in. Get your heart right. We try to fix up the
outside but the inside needs the most repair.
People are still tripping because they are not
applying the Word of God to their lives. If you
want God to bless you, you have to listen
attentively to the Word of God. You have to

hearken to the voice of the Lord that is coming from the man of God. If you don't listen, the devil will steal what you have left of the word of God right out of your heart. He will steal it and you won't even know it. You will start doing the opposite of what the word of God says. Let the word of God take root in your
heart and mind. People will fail God because they won't let the word of God take root in their heart. If the root of God does not take root in your heart you will flip. You will be walking around like a chicken with its head cut off. If you don't want to be saved it will not take root in you. If you want to be saved there is nothing that can stop you from living the word of God. Obedience to the word of God and the man of God will keep your mind.

The bible tells the sisters to obey their own husbands. If you do this the Bible calls you daughters of Sarah. We were born in the lineage of Abraham by faith. Sarah obeyed Abraham. You should want to please your husband. If you are not married you should learn this now and know it later. You are daughters of Sarah as long as you do well as it tells us in I Peter 3:6. The Bible also tells us men to dwell with our wives according to knowledge. You need to know what she can and can't take. It is not just your world. The word dwell means to live with. We need to love our wives and treat them right. This is for the married and the unmarried men. Learn each other as you go along. You cannot learn someone overnight. Knowledge has to be applied to all of our lives. It is a process. Some people haven't been married long enough to know one another. My wife and I have been married for thirty two years and I am still learning and finding out things. Honor your wife. She is not stupid. You cannot be a male chauvinist. You are both heirs together of the grace of life. If you get anything in your heart your prayers will be hindered and the heavens will be like brass where your prayers will bounce right off of it. My wife is my queen. I must talk to her like a queen. She must respect me. She must talk to me like a king. If I talk to her silly then the people will talk to her like that.

Cook your husband a breakfast and don't put anything in it. Sometimes you have to get mad at yourself and say, "No, I am not going to do it." You can make your own life bitter by being mean. It is up to the husband and wife to make their own lives sweet. The wife can take so much stress off her husband with a simple neck and back rub. The husband can do the same thing. It is up to the woman to keep the house clean. The harlot gets the man by spraying fragrances on the bed. She keeps things nice. He might not get that at home. When he goes over there, he's stuck like a bug in a spider web. The same goes for the husband. If you smell all the time and you don't like to wash yourself there will be a man somewhere with good smelling cologne on. After you have worked all day, jump in the shower. Take care of your oral hygiene. These things need to be taken care of. You wonder why she pulls away from you when you try to kiss her. It's not that she doesn't want to kiss you, it's just that your breath is not smelling great at that time.  You need to handle that problem.  You should not try to kiss your husband or wife with bad breath.

I Peter 3:1-7 reads, "Likewise ye wives, be in subjection to your own husbands; that if any obey not the word, they also may without the word be won by the conversation of the wives; while they behold their chaste conversation coupled with fear.  Whose adorning let it not be that outward adorning of plaiting the hair and wearing of gold or putting on of apparel; but let it be the hidden man of the heart, in that which is not corruptible and the ornament of the meek and quiet spirit, which is in the sight of God of great price.  For after this manner in the old time the holy women also, themselves, being in subjection unto their own husbands; even as Sarah obeyed Abraham, calling him Lord; whose daughters ye are, as long as ye do well and are not afraid with amazement. Likewise ye husbands, dwell with them according to knowledge, giving honour unto the wife as the weaker vessel and as being heirs together of the grace of life that your prayers be not hindered."

# Train Up a Child

You can't do what you want in front of the community. Somebody is watching you. People in the community are watching you saying, "Don't they go to church?" You can lose your influence because your child is lying and saying wrong things and because you think your child is an angel you will believe it and try to beat somebody up.

We have to stop taking up for our bad children and we know they are bad. If you are in a situation where there were children already there when you married each other the mother or father that was already there should make the children obey the parent that is coming in. Just because my wife had nieces and nephews living with us didn't mean they didn't obey me. I might not be their biological father but I am the one that raised them. You cannot take sides. Never be partial. You will cause them to hate their stepfather or stepmother and won't know why. I treat my stepchildren just like they are my own with no special treatment. Some man married a woman with teenagers and tried to come in and command things. They weren't hearing it. They were already smelling themselves. It doesn't work like that. You have to treat them with kindness. If you do they will love you forever. Teach your children to say, "Yes Maam" and "Yes Sir". That is respect. A lot of children have been shipped to their fathers and the fathers are angry. One father told his child's mother that she would never see her children again because she wrecked his life when she dropped them off to him and left.

Young people, obey your parents in all things. Fathers don't make your children angry. Don't tease them. You will make them mean and angry. Don't provoke them to anger. You will discourage them. If you overcorrect your children you will make them weak individuals.

If children obey their parents then God is pleased. He tells the fathers not to provoke or aggravate their children. You can't pick with them. You will make them mad, angry and mean. They will not function right in school because you are picking on them at home. I didn't go around my house teasing and picking with my children. They were often scared to ask me things. Not because I was mean but because I was always sleeping because I worked third shift. I did not want them asking for anything while I was sleeping. Children can't see what you see now. When they grow up they will refer back to what you told them.

Fathers don't provoke your children to anger. You will have them grow up and not want to work. You cannot badger your children. Especially your boys. You will make sissies out of them. They will grow up to hate you. You don't want your children to hate you. You must tell them the right thing and let them go. I had to come to realize that my children were getting older and I can't keep them at home all their lives. We want them to be saved but we have to let them fly. I learned from my oldest son, Michael, Jr. You love them but you don't want to let them go. I would see them on the corner and blow at them. I stopped trying to preach to them and telling them they need to be saved. If you keep doing that it will put rebellion in them. I had to stop doing that. When I stopped, they started coming in the church. Stop badgering them and telling them they are going to hell. If they were raised in the church then they know. You can't always tell them what to do and they are grown. You can't bully them. Let them get their own personalities. I tried to make my sons be like me. I had to realize that they are individuals. Even my twins are individuals. They have to make decisions on their own. That does not mean that they can't come to me for advice. I have more wisdom and knowledge than they do. I've been around the block a few times and I know some things. They know they are doing wrong. Preacher's kids are sometimes the worse ones. The devil wants to get the head, so he works on our sons. Some of your children might not be saved, but you just live the life before them and soon enough they will be.

All of our young people are not in the streets. Let them be young people. They are not smoking marijuana, running the streets, drinking or clubbing. Leave them alone. God will get you. You were once young. That is why we need activities in the church. They don't want to be in church twenty four hours a day, seven days a week. We don't even want to be in church that much. When it is time for Bible Class that is what it is going to be. Take them out bowling and skating. It is not a sin. Let them play on basketball teams. When they learn how to work on a team they will be preparing themselves to work on a job. They will be team players. Whey they get married they will learn how to be a team with their spouse. There is no I in team. A team is a group of people that strategize together.

We get angry when things don't go right around the house. Some of you can't relate to that because your children are below your knees.

They leave everything out. They don't clean up after themselves. The ants or roaches or both are crawling around and you can never find time to get your house the way you want it.

You are supposed to whip your child at the point of disobedience, not when you are full of anger. Then at that point you want to half way kill them. Put them on a punishment and leave them there. Video games and television are not punishment. Take the television away and take away their privileges and they will start obeying you. Take away things they like to do. Make them go to their rooms and do their homework.

Children are the best manipulators there are. They will play one parent against the other. They will go ask momma something and she will say no. When they go to daddy he says yes. You have to communicate with each other and keep down the friction. You can't say, "Yes you can because your daddy doesn't know." What you do develops good or bad character in your children. I used to tell my children not to ask me anything while I am asleep. I might tell them anything. A son that does foolish things are a destruction to his father. Whatever you do is a reflection on your parents. Proverbs 19:13 says, "A foolish son is the calamity of his father; and the contentions of a wife are a continual dropping."

I thought I was a man at seventeen and decided to move out of my mother's house. Life is not easy when you move out on your own. You have to pay the rent, feed yourself and pay for the phone that you are yapping on. If you don't pay your bills you will be right back where you started. I love my mother but I was not going back to her house. I would look real silly going back home at forty eight years old. Some things you just can't do.

We have to learn to let our children fly. Children who are born in church are very sheltered. I have been guilty of not letting some of my children fly. You want to do all you can for them and sometimes deplete yourself. There are times when you have to put on the brakes. My wells are kind of dry now. Not only from my children but other people's grown children. Don't get me wrong, I don't mind helping anyone. If I had money like I want to I would help anyone who needs to be helped. I am blessed today because I help people.

Our young people need prayer because the spirits in this world are still pulling them while they are in the church. The world is a dangerous place and the devil will make you do dangerous things.

God has been good to my children. They have been out there and know what it is like. The devil will get you out there and make you think you are Butch Cassidy and the Sundance Kid. There were people who would murder their own brothers. The devil will provide for you just to keep you out there. One of my sons told me that he had fifty dollars and he gambled it and ended up with twenty five hundred dollars. If they are being provided for by the devil they don't want to come to church and get a hamburger job. They are making big money out there. That is why we need to have programs to get them off the streets. These young men and women are driving BMW's, Lincolns and SUV's. It takes years to get things like that without selling drugs. The church is going to have to do more than jump and shout. We are living in a different age than when I was a little boy growing up. We need to pray that God will bring our young people in and keep them in. There is nothing on the street but death and destruction. The devil will let you have fun for a while. That is why it is good to have extracurricular activities. We can't make them sit in church all the time.

We need to pray for our young people that are in the streets. They need to know that you don't have to be doing anything to get hurt or killed these days. That is why it is best to stay in the church and give your life to the Lord. There is nothing out there but death, hell and destruction.

There is a spirit that draws you out to the streets. It is a struggle between two worlds. Our young people are pressured to go in the streets. Don't allow anyone to pressure you into selling drugs or doing anything that you know is not the right thing to do. You have to make your own decisions about the life that you want for yourself. You have to see that God wants to use you for His glory. A lot of times things have to happen for people to wake up and see that the way they are going is the wrong way. We need to pray that God will keep our children. The church life is a good life. Don't let anyone tell you that you are too young to be saved. It is a good thing to be young and save in the church. You don't have to go out there and sell yourself to the devil. It is not worth losing your soul.


One more thought for parents:

Don't be afraid to tell your children no. One person asked me if they should go to a rap concert for their birthday. I told them no. Those kinds of places carry spirits. The lyrics that they sing carry spirits. If you let them listen to it in your house, your house will have spirits in it. Even if they are not saved, if they are living in your house you need to take control. Let them move out and listen to it in their own house. The devil doesn't want our young people to be saved. Don't let the devil trick our young people. Some people make mistakes so other people can learn from it. If you have never been out in the world learn from somebody else's mistakes and don't ever go out there.

This is just to encourage the parents to let you now that if your children are out there in the land of the living, God can and will bring them back.

# **The New Man**

Don't be a thief. Get out of your mother and
your wife's purse. Stop stealing on the job.
Taking toilet paper and light bulbs from your job
is not what saints are supposed to do. That's what
the store is for. You will go to prison for twenty
years for a roll of toilet paper. Don't you see how
the devil tricks us.

In Matthew 15:13, Jesus said, "Every plant,
which my heavenly Father hath not planted shall
be rooted up." Everybody that Jesus did not plant
is not a child of God. The Bible speaks about the
children of the wicked one. The devil has
children too. He also has stepchildren.
Backsliders are stepchildren. When they turn
from God the devil adopts them. Everybody that
is not in God shall be rooted up. Don't worry
about the Pharisees and the religious leaders.
Leave them alone. If the blind lead the blind we

will be walking around with no one able to see and we will fall into a ditch. I don't want anyone that can't see try to lead me anywhere, whether it be spiritually or naturally. The Bible calls the prophets of old, Seer's. They were able to see into the future and see bad things before they happened and warn people. That is what I am doing now. I am warning the people. When the preacher is preaching, people would often say that he is not talking to them but he is talking to everyone else. People always want to point the finger at other people and say that it is not them, but in reality it is them. You are the man, you are the woman. Don't walk like the Gentiles walked, which means don't walk like other men or women walk. Don't act like sinners. You are sanctified. In other words you don't walk like sinners walk. You don't live like sinners live. These people live by the foolishness of their mind (vanity). Sinner can't see God like you can see him. They can't see him because of the blindness of their heart and the blindness of their mind. They are past feeling and have given themselves to lasciviousness or all types of lust with all uncleanness and greasiness.

Ephesians 4:20-21 says, "But ye have not so learned Christ; if so be that ye have heard him, and have been taught by him, as the truth is in Jesus." You are being taught by Christ through the man of God. The truth is in Jesus and not in Mohammed. It is not in Harry Krishna neither is it in Mussolini. It is definitely not in Saddam Hussein or Bin Laden. The truth is and will always be in Jesus.

In the book of Ephesians 4:22 it reads, "That ye put off concerning the former conversation of the old man, which is corrupt according to the deceitful lusts." The word conversation is in the way you talk or the way you live. You shouldn't act like you did when you were in the world. Be renewed and get your mind right. What's on your mind? Put on the new man, which is Jesus. He is the new man.

You should surround yourself with good, credible men and women. People with progression on their mind. What's on your mind? Whether we know it or not we progress everyday.

We get older, our hair gets grayer and our body changes. We sometimes get shorter. It's all apart of a changing process. You don't have all your teeth, your hair recede, your blood pressure is all out of whack and now everything gets on your nerves. You keep night lights on to go to sleep and we keep baseball bats and sticks by our beds. What's on your mind? We change one way or the other. We think more mature now. We don't think like we did when we were eighteen. At least I hope not.

Titus 1:7 tells us to be sober. Being sober means to be stable in our minds. Your thoughts must be serious and not silly when it comes to God's work. That doesn't mean to walk around looking silly all the time. That is not soberness.

Titus 1:9-16 says, "Holding fast the faithful word as he hath been taught, that he may be able by sound doctrine both to exort and to convince the gainsayers. For there are many unruly and vain talkers and deceivers, especially they of the circumcision: whose mouths must be stopped,

who subvert whole houses, teaching things which
they ought not, for filthy lucre's sake. One of
themselves, even a prophet of their own, said, the
Cretians are always liars, evil beasts, slow bellies.
This witness is true. Wherefore rebuke them
sharply, that they may be sound in the faith; not
giving heed to Jewish fable, and commandments
of men, that turn from the truth. Unto the pure all
things are pure: but unto them that are defiled and
unbelieving is nothing pure; but even
their mind and conscience is defiled. They
profess that they know God; but in works they
deny him, being abominable, and disobedient and
unto every good work reprobate." When you get
rebuked, it is not to make you run out of the
church but it is to make you sound in the truth.
When you are rebuked sharply you need to say it
is for your good that you may be sound and not
silly. To people who are pure, all things are pure.
People who have stuff in them think that
everybody is like them. When people steal they
think that you are doing it too. They don't think
anybody can live holy. Everybody is not doing
filth. They say they know God but through their

works they deny them. Their minds are messed up. What's on your mind?

Jeremiah 17:5-10 reads, "Thus saith the Lord; cursed be the man that trusteth in man, and maketh flesh his arm and whose heart departeth from the Lord. For he shall be like the heath in the desert, and shall not see when good cometh; but shall inhabit the parched places in the wilderness, in a salt land and not inhabited. Blessed is the man that trusteth in the Lord, and whose hope the Lord is. For he shall be as a tree planted by the waters, and that spreadeth out her roots by the river, and shall not see when heat cometh, but her leaf shall be green; and shall not be careful in the year of drought, nether shall cease from yielding fruit. The heart is deceitful above all things and desperately wicked: who can know it? I the Lord search the heart, I try the reins, even to give every man according to his ways, and according to the fruit of his doings. Men will let you down as the fifth verse tells us. His flesh is his strength or leaning post. There are people who are trees but they are not planted by the living water. They are planted by other things. The scriptures tell us that there are rivers of water that supply. If a river is not moving and stagnated then it will begin to stink. Things will die in it. God puts his trees on rivers that supply water to them. God wants his church (or leaves) to be green and full of life, not dried up or dead. After Christ died, he rose again that we might live. We are lively stones in the building. You are to yield fruit when things look dry in your life because you have the Holy Ghost. The fruits of the spirit are to be evident in our lives. The tough times are when we are to yield fruit.

When I came out of the world I stopped hanging with the people I used to hang with. Those relationships are over because I am saved now. I don't care how much of good friends we were. They will start cursing and sometimes say sorry, but after a while they will keep on cursing because they are used to your presence. You can't send forth sweet and bitter water at the same time. It has to be one or the other. You can't be saved and a sinner at the same time. We don't want the mentality of keep falling and getting up. The word of God tells us that He is able to keep us from falling. The only way He can keep us from falling is if we stop tripping. Leave the world alone. You don't have to fall. Are we calling God a liar when He says that he can keep us from falling and present us faultless? Either you believe it or you don't. You keep falling because you want to fall. If you obey the word of the Lord you won't fall.

# The Fear of God

People who don't have peace want to war all the time. They have no fear before God. You can kind of understand that in the world, but there should not be warring in the church. Our battle is not with each other but with spiritual wickedness and the principalities of the air.

People don't have fear for the man of God. I wasn't afraid of my pastor but I feared him. I had respect for him. I walked around him like I was walking on eggshells. He was the man of God. If you look at your man of God any other way than being the man of God you will miss your blessing. You will miss your anointing. You cannot disrespect the man of God. He made the pastor the overseer. Not the whip lasher. I have to be careful how I feed the flock. Acts 20:25-29 says, "And now, behold, I know that ye all, among whom I have gone preaching the kingdom of God, shall see my face no more.  Wherefore I take you to record this day, I am pure from the blood of all men.  For I have not shunned to declare to you all the counsel of God.  Take heed therefore unto yourselves, and to all the flock, over which the Holy Ghost hath made you overseers, to feed the church of God, which he hath purchase with his own blood.  For I know this, that after my departing shall grievous wolves enter among you, not sparing the flock."  The correlative scripture to Acts is I Peter 2:2-4 which says, "Feed the flock of God which is among you, taking the oversight thereof, not by constraint, but willingly; not for filthy lucre, but of a ready mind; neither as being lord over God's heritage, but being ensamples to the flock.  And when the chief Shepherd shall appear, ye shall receive a crown of glory that fadeth not away."

People have no fear of God anymore.  They walk out of church when they want to.  They come in when they want to.  They support songfests and concerts and not the church.  I go to songfests and concerts but not when church is going on. People do not respect the man that God places in the pulpit. I am a pastor that will not tell you anything wrong. I was not trained or groomed that way. My pastor would travel to Kentucky and tell other pastors that he was grooming me. God is not going to put a man/woman of God over you that is crazy. He will put someone there that will help you but you have to want to be helped. What good is going to the doctor and you keep pulling away from him? You might as well stay home. Every time you go to the hospital they have to catch you to give you a shot. You are wasting their time. You drop your car off at the auto shop to get it fix but tell the mechanics not to work on your car. It makes no sense to come to the church and not want to be helped. All of us need God to help us. From the pulpit to the back door. The church is the emergency room. The church is Christ's hospital where we can come to be healed, saved and delivered. The devil has been trying to destroy us so we come to the house of God so he can fix us.

You don't naturally eat once a day. Most people eat three times a day. You can't go all year without drinking water. Why come to church and not get anything out of it?

Psalms 36:1 says, "The transgression of the wicked within my heart, that there is no fear of God before his eyes." That shouldn't be in the church. When the preacher is preaching you shouldn't say, "I don't care what he/she says." You have no fear of God in your heart.

Luke 23:39-40 reads, "And one of the malefactors which were hanged railed on him, saying, "If thou be Christ, save thyself and us." But the other answering rebuked him, saying, "Dost not thou fear God, seeing thou art in the same condemnation?" How can you talk to Jesus like that and we are on the cross being crucified with him? We are all in the same boat together. How can you say something against someone and your life isn't worth two dead flies? We have storms in all of our lives. You might get the wind and I might get the rain but it is still a storm.

In the closing of this book, it is my prayer that you have identified the works of the flesh and that you also have the spiritual tools to help you obtain the fruits of the spirit to live a long and prosperous life that God has planned for you.

The next few pages are for you to take notes while reading to jot down your thoughts and work on the areas that you need to improve on. God bless you and may heaven smile upon you is my prayer.

# Notes

(for your thoughts, improvements and goals)

_____

_____

_____

_____

_____

_____

_____

_____

_____

_____

_____

_____

_____

_____

_____

_____

_____

_____

_____

_____

_____

_____

# Notes

(for your thoughts, improvements and goals)

_____

_____

_____

_____

_____

_____

_____

_____

_____

_____

_____

_____

_____

_____

_____

_____

_____

_____

_____

_____

_____

_____

_____

# Notes
(for your thoughts, improvements and goals)

_____

_____

_____

_____

_____

_____

_____

_____

_____

_____

_____

_____

_____

_____

_____

_____

_____

_____

_____

_____

_____

_____

_____

_____

# Notes
(for your thoughts, improvements and goals)

Made in the USA
Monee, IL
10 May 2020